About *Life Lessons: A Connection of Souls Throughout Life's Journey*

"Her assignments made us look into our hearts and souls."

—Mary Alice Bottegal Wise

"Her teaching instilled a love of grammar in me… and I have passed that love on to my own students over the past 28 years of teaching."

—Karen Moore-Soto

"Oh, my, did she ever make an impact on my life. Let me count the ways."

— Attorney Francesca Carinci

"Her students were smiling because she was there… There was never a student she did not like. ..She was tough on some, but always clear of what the intention was and quite fair. She demanded excellence from us, and we, in turn, were inspired to seek that excellence."

—Judith Coopy, author and poet, *My Little Boy*

"She is still an inspiration to me."

—Veronica Furka Pollus, CCHS 1973

"She was bright and enthusiastic and curious…a dynamic combination."

—Cindy Shimko Guerrieri, CCHS 1973-74

"She taught us to value ourselves, work hard, and gave me a love of reading that I still enjoy."

—Pam Johnson Maroon

"If I've learned anything in these last twenty years of university teaching, I probably got it from Dr. Sunyoger. Mary Antoinette is the consummate professional: loving, tough, incredibly engaged. And she does it all with joy. That's the thing that comes through. So, if you want to become a better teacher (and who doesn't), or if you just want to be entertained, to be brought closer to the things that matter, read *Life Lessons*. You will be a better person for having done so."

—Dr. David Craig, author of *Mary's House*

LIFE
LESSONS

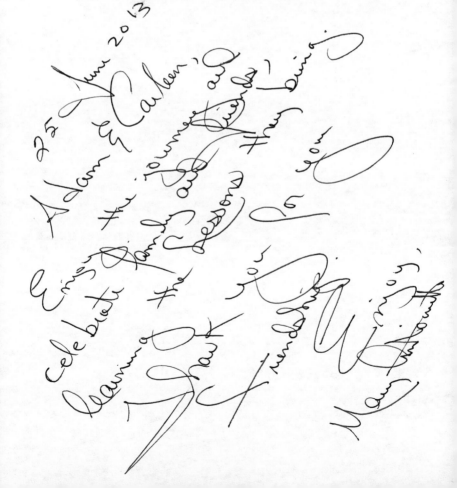

LIFE
LESSONS

*A Connection of Souls
Throughout Life's Journey*

MARY ANTOINETTE GALLO SUNYOGER, PH.D.

TATE PUBLISHING
AND ENTERPRISES, LLC

Published by Tate Publishing & Enterprises, LLC
127 E. Trade Center Terrace | Mustang, Oklahoma 73064 USA
1.888.361.9473 | www.tatepublishing.com

Tate Publishing is committed to excellence in the publishing industry. The company reflects the philosophy established by the founders, based on Psalm 68:11,
"The Lord gave the word and great was the company of those who published it."

Book design copyright © 2013 by Tate Publishing, LLC. All rights reserved.
Cover design by Rodrigo Adolfo
Interior design by Mary Jean Archival
Illustrations by Richard M. Sunyoger, AIA, LEED AP

Published in the United States of America

ISBN: 978-1-62510-429-8
1. Biography & Autobiography / Educators
2. Education / Teaching Methods & Materials / Language Arts
13.05.28

Dedication

I dedicate this book to my parents, who laid my life's foundation with a solid faith in God and an eternal love for my family. My parents sacrificed for me so that I could go to college and earn a degree in a profession that I would never consider a job. For this, I shall never forget their gift of self.

I dedicate this book to my brother and sister who have shared their lives with mine from the moment of birth, who have enjoyed a beautiful childhood with me, and who have shared in the pain and laughter with me.

I dedicate this book to my husband who unselfishly supported me throughout my MA and PhD process. Without his love for and belief in me, I would not be where I am today.

I dedicate this book to my son who watched me struggle as I balanced the roles of being a mother, teacher, and doctoral student when he was young. I pray to this day that he recognized that my role as his mother was the most important one—and still is.

I dedicate this book to my grandson and granddaughter who helped me look at life in a new way, an innocent way with laughter and play. They gave me another reason to live my life well, leaving a legacy of truth, beauty, and goodness so that they, too, will learn to live their lives to the fullest.

I dedicate this book to my students, for they are the ones who molded me into the teacher I am today.

Because of them I continue to teach. Because of them I live a life of peace. For them I thank God.

My students sustained and still sustain my passion for teaching. They ignite my enthusiasm, humility, and love each and every time I walk into a classroom. My students and I have given one another a portion of our lives, spending time in a room where knowledge is pursued and shared. My students and I have shared our lives, connecting them with one another. We have left a legacy of goodness with one another. We have become better individuals because of one another. We journeyed through life together, holding one another's hand while protecting one another's soul.

For this I thank God, for He has given me so many blessings. This has been a great life, one I shall live to its fullest for the goodness of others. I thank God for His gift of faith. I thank God for His gift of family. I thank God for His gift of students.

Acknowledgments

If I acknowledged everyone who has contributed to the final step in this process of writing this book, I would have volumes of names. My life has been blessed with all of these individuals who have formed me into the woman I am today. But for this moment, I would like to thank Fr. Brian Cavanaugh, TOR, for pushing me to become "bodacious," thrusting me into the first step of the publication process. I thank my colleague Dr. David Craig, who is in the Department of English with me and who took time to read a few of these chapters. For her expertise in Library Research, I thank Kathleen Donohue for assisting me with the citation information. Through their persistence and consistent response to my cry for help with some computer issues, I thank Sandi Radvansky and her team at Franciscan University of Steubenville.

I thank Franciscan University of Steubenville for granting me my requested sabbatical so that I could finish this book. I thank my husband who believed in my dreams moreso than I, my son who blessed me with a look at life in a new and miraculous way, and my grandson, Landon, and granddaughter, Gabriella, who accepted me for just being their "Nanny" and for giving me their innocent and infinite love. I thank my family for their patience while I found hiding places in the shapes of libraries, my university office, and my "secret" places in my home so that I could write for hours. I thank my now deceased parents who gave me the confidence to reach my dreams and who gave me—through great sacrifice—a college education to begin the first step. I pray that they are looking down on me with a smile full of love and satisfaction.

I thank my brother who gave me the idea to frame my book this way and who took time to read my book, commenting: "Very touching. Your last chapter is beautiful. I could see Mommy beaming at you in her seat. Beautiful message, and it touched me deeply... I can't believe you flunked Mommy!"

I thank my sister who gave me her "ear" whenever I needed a best friend to listen and who told me that she couldn't stop crying when she read my manuscript, saying that her favorite line is at the end of the book: "Mom was ready to catch her falling star and pin it to the sky."

That's my favorite line, too.

I thank my former professors who, so long ago, gave me the foundation of academic preparation for this work. I thank every single student whom I ever taught during these past forty-one years: each student has given me the experience, the wisdom, the courage, and the passion to pursue my vocation with eagerness, love, and excitement. Each student has given me these stories of life and learning.

And most of all, I thank God for giving me this life and all who have been a part of it. These individuals have offered me the opportunity to grow, to flourish, and to jump out of bed every morning with excitement to live another day of life. These individuals have offered me the opportunity to lay my head on my pillow every night, thanking God for such a blessed day. When my father lived with me during his final stages of Alzheimer's, we would say the Our Father together every night. I recited the prayer for him, since he couldn't remember the once-familiar words. This was our ritual. And at the end of the Our Father, my Dad would sit for a few moments, looking at me with eyes that revealed the Dad I knew lying somewhere below the Alzheimer's devastation, and would say very slowly, "Thank you. Thank you. I had a beautiful day."

And I would respond, "Good, Daddy. Good. And what was your favorite part of the day, Daddy?"

Speaking with his eyes and soul, he would say, "Being with you, doll. Being with you."

To my students, I say thank you. Thank you. I had a beautiful day. It was beautiful from being with you.

Contents

Prologue

This is a little book of true stories. Each chapter is a narrative of one student who taught me a lesson when, ironically, I thought I was the only one in the class teaching a lesson. The lesson learned from each narrative may not be profound and philosophical information, but it is a life lesson, one that you could capture through some detail, even a sliver of meaning—some point that could guide your thinking, acting, and responding in both your personal, professional, and educational experiences—the way it has meaningfully guided me throughout these years. As we meet the many individuals throughout our lives, do we take the time to connect, to find meaning in that connection, and to learn from it?

Yes, these are narratives that I do not want to forget and never will; therefore, I have written them in order to share these stories with you. If one story in any way touches your heart and enables you to be more effective in the classroom, to be a better person in life, to exhale from your struggles and to appreciate the life God has given you, then this little book of stories has achieved its purpose.

My love for teaching and for my students—both past, present, and future—has enriched my life and has given me the fire and courage to walk into the classroom and into life. No other profession offers me the fulfillment that teaching has given me; no other profession challenges me; no other profession ignites my passion for life. And for that I offer my memories to the lives of those who have influenced me and who will carry the torch by touching others' lives.

I thank those students who are the "characters" in these stories; I also thank those students who are not in the book but who are in my life. You have taught me well, dear students. And for this I am indebted. I simply hope that I have used these life lessons that you have taught me and that I continue to use them. May your lives be as blessed as mine has been. May you never work a day in your life because you have the passion for what you do in the vocation that you choose. May you be open to the lessons that those around you are teaching you.

May you share them well so that others may learn.

God bless,
Mary Antoinette Gallo Sunyoger, Ph.D.

CHAPTER 1

My First Day

My First-Year Junior English Class's Story

"Let's see how long this one lasts" is what I heard echoing throughout the classroom as I confidently—a feigned confidence, that is—walked into my high school junior English class. Four years of undergraduate work at a local college (now a university) did not fully prepare me for the journey I was about to take, like a captain who thinks that all is ready and that all is battened down for a smooth sail, but, instead, tackles storms and rough waters. My mind was ready; my heart was steady, but the comment from the student in the first seat, middle row, threw me overboard—overboard for the rest of that day's journey that I was so enthusiastic to begin.

Tony really was a good guy, I realized, after I taught him for the entire year, but that day proclaimed a different edict: Tony is the leader of this group and has predicted that the teacher will stay temporarily, and during that stay, she will not be a happy passenger on this trip.

I learned the students' names that day; I presented an overview of the course material that would be covered—American literature, composition, and grammar. There would be some speeches given, since I was (and still am) a true believer in language arts and the need for students to have a command of standing in front of a group (no matter how large or how small) and speaking with clarity, conciseness, and effectiveness. As I learned throughout my own continued schooling, the ancient rhetors believed that delivery was the key component in the art of rhetoric; in fact, the importance of delivering a speech is the ingredient for an audience to stop, linger, and listen—even being affected by the body language, voice inflection, and, of course, the arrangement, invention, and style of the speech.

So there I stood—behind my navigational wheel. There my students sat, not too ready to begin their journey with me. For me to be there took many hours of hard study and solitary nights; for me to be there demanded continuous sacrifice on the part of my parents. And I was sticking around for a long time. The cost of a college education per semester (back then) was a fraction of the cost of what it is today; wages were unlike what they are today. My parents scraped to meet the four-hundred-and-fifty dollar tuition that was raised every semester, reaching the height in my last semester of six-hundred-and-fifty dollars. I am certain, however, that there are parents today who would gladly exchange their tuition payments with those of my parents.

The fifty-two-minute period took forever with those juniors that day. There were thirty-two students, most of them male. I mean—most of them were the football team! Dave was the captain of the high school team; Tony was the quarterback; Chris and Johnny were linemen. Yes, there were some females in that class, but they were subdued and made quite sullen by the testosterone in that class. Years later, one of the female students whom I never really had a chance to meet came back as my substitute teacher for my high school classes when I took my maternity leave. I am still proud of her and of her professional life.

There were many students during my first-year of teaching. Each one tested me; rather, I tested myself as I searched for my strengths and my limitations. Some I found; some I never did find that year.

But I survived.

Life Lesson Learned

I learned that persistence kept me in the classroom and that faith and confidence were the vehicles driving me throughout that first year and are still the vehicles that drive me throughout my life..

For this life lesson, I thank you, my first-year junior English class.

CHAPTER 2

Smiles and Frowns

My First-Year Freshman English Class and Mike's Story

The wind slapped my face with compassionless hands of ice. I couldn't thaw that smile that perched on my frozen lips. My stomach was sick; I was perspiring. (*Don't ever let them see you sweat* rang somewhere in my head as I looked at the sea of faces.) No class in my BA program of study prepared me for the myriad of emotions that I was feeling that first day.

This is my first class! I have six more freshman classes waiting to board as they begin this year of their journey with me.

I did begin seven journeys that first day. Each port held at least thirty students who waited to board and sail the sea of learning with me, and there was room for each student. Some were quite eager; others were quite hesitant, and some were unwilling. But begin we did.

My planning period was fourth period, so I had fifty-two minutes (in addition to doing the work nightly) to grade papers or to review or to plan my classes. I had my English lecture notes on eight-and-a-half-by-eleven legal yellow tablet paper, and I was ready, I thought.

I wasn't.

I prepared for a fifty-two minute class, finding out that the yellow legal sheets took only twenty-five minutes of teaching instead. My panic was in the twenty-five minutes I had left. *Do I sing, dance, tell stories, or simply give the students the rest of the class to do whatever they want?* The last option was definitely out; the first played a close second to that. The methodology used was to review the notes that were just given.

It worked! Surprisingly, the students reviewed the first twenty-five minutes of notes, checking their notebooks, adding what was missed and correcting what was wrong.

The junior class was soon over, and the freshman classes were approaching. The numbers were unfathomable. Every desk was taken—in every class period. This would be the challenge. No one back then told me that a risk-free environment was key in any class (as the education theorists Kirby, Kirby, and Liner state[i]). I was so far removed from that environment in my classroom. The risk-free environment would come a few years later, since during my first couple of years of teaching I couldn't smile and enjoy my students. I was too busy trying to survive.

"Never smile or be nice in the beginning of the school year. You can always let up toward the end of the academic year, but if you are friendly and smile, you will be unable to let up at the end of the year. This will create a situation where students will walk all over you." I couldn't shake those words pounding in my head. So…

I listened. I exuded no personality that was warm or welcoming—for a while.

In fact, a former freshman at Catholic Central High School stated forty years later:

> I learned that sometimes putting the fear of God and/or Ms. Gallo [my maiden name] in your lesson plan can be very effective! What I learned in your class was not so much about English but rather about respect. You were a very good teacher. You were a little tough on us sometimes, but in hindsight, you had to be. Now forty years later, I am proud to say that I brought with me many of those lessons learned about respect, and as a result I am very proud of the people our girls have become. Thanks, Ms. G.!
>
> —Mike, Facebook, December 21, 2011

The comment made me smile when I received it and still makes me smile. I did not realize that I was teaching respect as faith upholds—respect for the human person. I was too preoccupied trying to memorize the notes for my class lectures. In fact, I did not even realize that there were students in the classroom during that first year of teaching! That's how preoccupied I was.

I was too busy reading my notes, worrying about making a mistake, wondering if the day would ever come when I would walk into a classroom—being myself—and not constantly refer to lecture notes in front of the class. I wanted to talk *with* the students instead of talking *at* them. Every night I prayed for the day when my heart would quit pounding from fear and when the frown would metamorphose into a smile—a genuine smile. I wanted to share my love and passion for teaching. But I wore no smile when I walked into my classroom during the first couple of years. I prayed for the day when I could reflect my love and passion for teaching with others—especially with my students.

Life Lesson Learned

I learned that there are human beings in the classroom. And when working with human beings, teachers should know that it isn't about knowing the notes perfectly; it's about recognizing the human person and dignifying that person. The curly, thick-black-haired freshman with an inviting smile taught me that. Being ME in the classroom is what my students want. They want someone who reciprocates humanity and respect—who recognizes THEM. This lesson wasn't learned right away—I had to continue the journey to understand.

For this life lesson, I thank you, Freshman English class and Mike.

CHAPTER 3

A Painful Memory

Jason's Story

My first year of teaching was such a hectic one: feeling uncomfortable in the new role of being the teacher and not the student, relearning old material in a new way in order to teach it, and learning new material in order to teach it became my constant companions. Truthfully, when I walked into that high school English classroom, I was so concerned about remembering my notes and not making a mistake that I would forget to look at my students, actually forgetting that they were part of the class! I prayed every night that I would reach the point where I could teach without constantly referring to my class notes and could look in the eyes of the students, recognizing their personhood.

That first year demanded so much of my time and energy. I wanted to do my best for my students—for each and every one of them. I loved teaching, even with the fear and the nervousness that went with beginning my professional life, but every now and then the recurring reflection of wondering if I made the right decision visited my innermost thoughts.

Those days have passed; so many have been lived since that first year of teaching. No longer do I have the lecture notes in front of me on long, legal, yellow sheets of paper. No longer do I avoid looking into the eyes of my students; no longer do I overly question my decisions made throughout my teaching days, although I, as a reflective practitioner, reflect over the teaching day. My years of teaching and experiences have given me some wisdom of knowing what to do. This knowledge is revered and valued. It gives me peace and a place to share my passion for literature and composition, for sharing the human condition. There are so many good memories of my teaching experiences.

But it was not always this way.

He was a freshman who sat in the first row by the wall, last seat in that row. This was my first year of teaching, and having quiet, catatonic students seemed to be a blessing back then. Why? Perhaps I was too unseasoned to complicate my teaching; all that I could do at first was to lecture. Asking if students had questions was quite fearful for me then. (I was afraid I did not have the answers. Now I appreciate those who engage in the dynamic dialogue that connects class lectures.) Jason did his work, took notes, and gave me his attention in class. I never had a problem with him.

Reflecting on Jason now, I really never gave myself a chance to know him.

During my first year of teaching, I introduced journaling to all of my classes: all six freshman classes and one junior class. Every night, students had either unfocused or focused writing entries. They responded to a news item that grasped their attention, or they responded to one of my topics (respectively).

At the end of each quarter, I collected the notebooks and lost entire weekends reading each entry and responding to it. As the years of teaching added up, I became more experienced with organizing my time and my assignments, but I was always inundated with the journals. But journaling was too important to remove from my writing activities; in fact, I had students engaged in journaling throughout my ten years of high school teaching and even now in my university teaching.

Still, I was so raw, so unseasoned, so new to the profession my first year that I thought that I was the grammar police and had to look for every mistake made, focusing on mechanics and not on content. So my first year I collected journals, circling and commenting on every misspelled word, every comma splice, every missing colon, every mechanical error imaginable. This is how I read the journal entries—that was then. Later I found that the approach I used back then was far from being the correct one. Grading these areas has its place, but with "first things first," content matters first.

Jason taught me that.

Before we left for the two-week Christmas break my first year, I collected the journals, graded them for mechanics and returned them, feeling "on top of the world" for having conquered yet another set of grading journals. Not reading the content but only focusing on the mechanics, I don't recall what those entries discussed. I think back periodically, trying to remember what Jason had written, trying over and over again to find his cry for help, but always ending with the same result—finding nothing, remembering nothing but the mechanics.

That January when we returned from Christmas vacation and were preparing for midterm exams, the principal made an announcement over the PA (public announcement) system. One of the students had died (committed suicide, as we found out later) during the Christmas season.

It was Jason!

Later, I heard so many details, although I did not and still do not know if they were the truth or the fabrication from so many individuals retelling the story.

But the one detail remained: Jason was no longer in my class. He submitted his journal to me, which I returned to him, before he left for Christmas break. He never missed an assignment.

More often than I would like, I think about Jason, wondering what I could have found in the content of his entries. But I did not focus on the content; instead, the mechanics were the mythical sirens that kept my attention.

Sadness and guilt emerge every time I think of Jason. I still wonder: *Could I have seen a cry for help? Could I have diverted this tragedy?*

This was an incident that occurred during the first few months of my teaching career. After all of these years, I hope that Jason has forgiven me for spending endless hours looking for his misplaced commas and for not paying attention to his voice—or maybe to his cry for help.

I'll never know.

Requiescat in pace.

Life Lesson Learned

Jason has been with me throughout these forty-one years of teaching. Thinking of him and praying for him to this day, I keep my focus on each and every student—what the student writes and reveals. Writing is therapy. Writing is discovery. But what a teacher needs to remember the most is to listen, to dignify students by listening to their voices. Perhaps a teacher, then, may help a student with a life struggle.

Checking punctuation and spelling won't help students with serious problems. Yes, we need to know writing mechanics in order to be clear with our written ideas, but teachers must be readers first and must read content. We must not consider just *how* journal entries are written but *what is written*. Reading and listening to another's ideas dignifies that person. As human beings, we are sensitive to and compassionate about this. I have *never* focused solely on mechanics since that tragedy.

For this life lesson, I thank you, Jason.

CHAPTER 4

The Risk-Free Classroom

Mara's Story

Louise Rosenblatt, a researcher and educator in the teaching of literature and composition, heralds: "Teaching is a moral activity."[ii] This has been one of my guiding principles in the classroom. Her motto is my motto. When I began my teaching career, I did not know this theorist, but one major lesson I learned was being morally responsible for my students. However, this lesson did not begin with my teaching; it began with my parents, who taught their three children that "you do unto others as you would have them do unto you." It began with my parents who taught us to respect others.

Coming from a household of first-generation Italian-Americans and having a father who was blue collar and who worked two jobs, we did not have money for the "finer things in life," but we still had everything a good family needs: love and family. It was never spoken, but it was always seen in the actions: *sempre famiglia*. I didn't know it then, but I grew into understanding this as I became older. This feeling I carried into my own classroom. I found that the students sitting in front of me on a daily basis (high school) or a three-day-a-week basis (university) were my family. We were a familial community. And that was the beginning of developing a life-long bond with my students.

We were family.

With the dynamic of family, I knew that these students had to feel loved, cared for, dignified, confident, and successful. These qualities were familiar to me. These are characteristics of a good family environment carried into the classroom dynamic supported by the researcher and philosopher Nell Noddings.[iii] But some of the students didn't come from good environments. During my first year of high school teaching, I taught seven classes. I remember so well. There were 182 students who walked into Room 207 daily: six freshman classes and one junior class. There was a planning period, but that wasn't enough time to create valleys in the mountains of papers waiting to be graded. There were other activities to tackle. Moderating the yearbook and the Future Teachers Club kept me quite busy. I wanted to do my best for these students for whom I was responsible and…

Worrying about my notes and never wanting to make a mistake were at the top of my list.

But I did make mistakes, and I learned from those errors.

In the midst of all of this was a lone ranger of a girl—Mara. She was a tall girl who didn't seem to fit in with the others, to carry herself like the others, or to dress like the others, even though the students wore uniforms. She never walked into the class with anyone; she was always alone. Her face was never graced by a smile; her lips were drawn on her face with a horizontal, single line; her eyes followed her footsteps. Her eyes avoided contact with another.

Mara was always alone.

I never thought about the education theory behind it; I just knew what was right, what was Christian, what one human being should do for another. Dignity for the human person was what was needed. Mara was a young freshman in high school who needed someone to recognize her and to address her as a person. Again, since this was my first year of teaching, I did not consciously think about the education theory and its connection to education practice; instead, the student simply needed a smile, a compliment, some recognition.

On a daily basis and for every class, even though there were only three minutes between classes, I stood by my classroom door and greeted each student by name. The difficult part was learning everyone's names. What I did was the following: with every class, I took the first day as the longest day for the "drill" and called the class list, repeated the name, and made a conscious effort to connect the name with the face, going row by row, repeating each name, and then challenging a student to repeat the names with me. This reinforced the names for me and for the class. Sometimes I would remember names that the student didn't; other times students would remember names that I couldn't. It was fun and humbling at the same time.

But it worked.

When students walked into class the next day, I started again with the roll call, stating that if I mentioned someone's name during the class that it was the repetition that helped me know the names more quickly. Although it took time, it worked.

So I learned the students' names in my freshman English class that first day and every first day since then.

And I learned Mara's name.

Every time Mara approached my classroom door, I made certain that I looked her in the eyes, commented on her hair, shoes, knee socks (the socks were the single factor that distinguished each female student, since they wore uniforms), and her beautiful smile (that I knew was in there somewhere). It took quite a while, but Mara began to return my smile, to look me in the eyes, to walk a little more confidently into the classroom—although she was always alone.

After her freshman English class, I never had Mara in any other English class again. But she is always on my mind, especially when I teach my university students about the importance of offering students a risk-free classroom environment and about the importance of recognizing each student.

Years later, I was standing in a grocery store line, waiting to check my groceries and be on my way, when I looked at the woman in front of me. There was some familiarity about her, although I couldn't clearly recall if or where I had ever met her. When I heard her voice and caught her full face instead of just a profile, I knew.

It was Mara, grown up, thirty-five-plus years older—but it was she.

Gathering courage to interrupt the routine of paying for groceries, I asked what her name was.

"Mara," she whispered.

What I saw was not the woman in front of me but the invisible girl, the shadow of the girl who first walked into my class. We talked about her children, her years, and her life, when suddenly her eyes became focused, reflecting the core of her soul.

"I never had the opportunity to thank you for what you did for me when I was a freshman in your English class, and you don't know how that changed my life."

She had come from an abusive home and was never treated with respect as a child. Both her mother and father did not pay attention to her and abused her verbally on a daily basis.

"There were times when they didn't know I existed," she told me that day.

I didn't realize the repercussion of the small compliments and the smiles I had offered her so many years ago. But my recognition of that young woman added to the confidence and the strength to continue her life with goals and with accomplishments.

"Sticks and stones will break my bones, but names will never hurt me" is a saying that I never believed. Names break a person's spirit, and that's worse than breaking bones. Medical research has proven that bones grow back stronger, but the spirit takes a long time to rebuild.

Sometimes it never does.

But Mara had the laughter in her eyes. She had the flicker in her smile. She had the aura of confidence that every human being should have. Her experiences catapulted her to that place of honor, of courage, of forging through life's challenges that sometimes seem too big to surmount. Yet the people placed at different intersections in life do make those differences.

We teachers are those forces in life that make differences. And without *any* doubt, we must recognize the responsibility of that power given to us to make or break the human spirit of an individual, no matter how young or how old.

When I was a child, my mother used to tell me that when I smiled the whole world smiled with me. And when I frowned, I frowned alone. These words stuck with me, even as I entered into my teaching profession.

A smile isn't that hard to do, but it demands a commitment to what we do and with whom we do it. Teachers are committed to the vocation of teaching their students, to the vocation of dignifying each and every one of them.

Life Lesson Learned

What I learned early in the year was that I couldn't worry about looking stupid (although that was a main concern), and I accepted the challenge of learning the names and faces of each and every student sitting in my classes. I was afraid of making mistakes, indicating that my memory might not be perfect. But I learned the names, giving each student the dignity of personhood. We were family. And I learned that each person is special.

For this life lesson, I thank you, Mara.

CHAPTER 5

Are You Ever Going to Smile?

Jimmy's Story

One day after school, Jimmy walked into my classroom and asked if he could talk with me. A high school football player and a member of my first-year high school junior English class, Jimmy was confident and secure about walking into my room in order to ask me *the* question. Reflecting on that particular afternoon, I am certain that Jimmy was not representing only himself; instead, he stood for the entire junior class—the class comprising most of the football team.

"What can I do for you, Jimmy?" In my first-year innocence, I incorrectly thought that he was asking for help concerning that day's class lesson.

Instead, I heard, "Miss Gallo, are you ever going to smile in class?"

I was both surprised and speechless. I asked him what he meant, giving me time to compose myself. *Never let them see you perspire or smile* echoed throughout my body. Somewhere in some college class, those words introduced themselves, or perhaps I just used that mantra as a safeguard. I was afraid!

During my first year of teaching, I remember praying every night *and* every day, asking the Lord to give me peace, to allow me to be myself, and to enable me to smile. I wanted my students to know that I enjoyed being with them, that I cared for their educational well-being, that I had a passion for what I did. But most of all, I wanted the students to know that I cared about them.

But I was afraid to reflect it then.

So when Jimmy asked me if I would ever smile in class, I looked right into his eyes and said, "Jimmy, would you smile if you were standing in front of *that* class, teaching you and your peers in *that* class?"

"No, Miss Gallo. I see your point."

Case closed. My answer was received and accepted. But I still had to contend with the butterflies every morning as I drove to school, with the racing of my heart as I parked my car, with the shallow breathing as I drew closer to my Room 207 that first year.

Life Lesson Learned

Having the courage to do what we know is moral and right determines the route to take. We must have courage to make decisions and to stand by those decisions, accepting the consequences that come with those choices. In other words, we must be honest in what we do and in revealing who we really are—our strengths and our weaknesses, our courage and our fears. Trying to be who we aren't just doesn't work; it did not work for me. That was a most uncomfortable lesson learned.

For this life lesson, I thank you, Jimmy.

CHAPTER 6

Ciao to Teaching

Vincenzo's Story

Grammar was my best friend, especially since my freshman year in high school.

Fr. Belfield taught the freshman English class and offered me the opportunity to begin a love affair with the English language. Father Belfield asked me to help students with their grammar. Walking from student to student during English class, checking over the grammar work, and explaining what was correct and what wasn't chartered a course for me. But my teaching didn't begin with freshman grammar.

When I was in seventh grade at St. Anthony School, several of my classmates emigrated from Italy. My grade school was Italian, Catholic, first-generation and second-generation Italian-Americans. Sister Mary Theresa would ask me to help the new Italian students with the English language. The room was large with wide, hardwood floors. Of course, the desks were nailed to the floor on runners, so each desk was stationed in its place. If a teacher wanted to form a circle with the desks, a horseshoe, a square, those options were out of the question.

The traditional paradigm of the transmission model was followed. Teachers were in the front of the room; students looked at the backs of their peers' heads. In the back of the seventh-grade classroom were two large bay windows, separated by the only door of the one-room building. The right bay window housed two desks, one for me, and the other for the new student. It was a stereo situation. Sister taught the class, while I tutored a student English.

Vincenzo was one of my students who knew very little English. He had just come to the United States from Italy and was a new student in our seventh grade class. My ear was attuned to the language, since my parents were both Italian and spoke the language fluently. Sister may have seen potential in me when she asked me to help Vincenzo with the English language.

Our tutorial sessions consisted of learning functional English vocabulary so that Vincenzo could acclimate to the class and to American society. This experience challenged me, yet I looked forward to teaching him. Being a seventh grader, I highly doubt if I thought about any education theory or practice. Instead, I simply enjoyed the experience of sharing my knowledge with another person.

That was so long ago, but I still remember being "the teacher" at such an early age and helping my "first student."

Every now and then, I see Vincenzo and his wife where I live. And with his melodious, Italian accent… he speaks to me using good English.

Life Lesson Learned

Having an opportunity present itself during early years of formation is a blessing. Being placed in a teaching position when I was in seventh grade gave me a small taste of what it was like to be a teacher. Vincenzo taught me that I really like to interact with individuals and to share my knowledge. He taught me that teaching is a vocation and that I would love every minute of it. Vincenzo taught me that it is necessary to respect another's culture as we prepare the person for a new world.

For this life lesson, I thank you, Vincenzo.

CHAPTER 7

Doing the Unthinkable

Lou's Story

I walked into the grammar portion of my freshman English curriculum, thinking that I knew the content area. What I didn't realize was that my high school students came from the grade school "feeder" schools and had eight years of grammar preparation and that they knew their grammar better than I. They studied terminology and word relationships. The incredible reality was that almost every student in that freshman English class came from grade schools that *concentrated* on grammar study.

One student, however, knew his grammar better than the rest—and much better than I.

Lou sat in the first row, first seat. He was a quiet freshman who did not explode with answers every time I asked a question. But when I did call on him, he answered and answered correctly. In fact, he never responded incorrectly. As I used the grammar language and as I tried to explain the relationships of words with other words, I realized that I did not understand grammar well enough to explain it to my students.

While teaching different grammar lessons, I would look toward the first row, first seat. Lou's questions were not meant to taunt me but were meant for clarification. He really seemed to love the language and its grammatical structure. His innocent curiosity, however, made me uncomfortable, so uncomfortable that I shall never forget the following classroom situation.

Teaching the four basic parts of speech was easy. The students and I knew the difference between verbs, nouns, adjectives, and adverbs; but the other grammar areas taught me humility.

When I began singular and plural possessive case, I taught the lesson wrong. Reflecting on that lesson, I always wonder how I did that, since I knew possessive case. Perhaps being a novice brought about nervousness? But whatever the reason was, I still made the mistake.

Actually, I made several big grammatical mistakes.

The singular possessive case and plural possessive case were presented backward, inside out, and upside down. In other words, I was wrong. Without questioning me, Lou and the other students took their notes and left when the bell rang.

I knew that I had made a mistake—several mistakes—yet I was too proud to admit it. I dismissed the class and immediately began fretting over the course of action I needed to pursue. *Every teacher must be a reflective practitioner so that teachers can become more effective in the classroom* pounded throughout my body. I remembered those words from my college classes.

But what I thought about doing instead was to leave well enough alone and have the students learn possessive case the following year—or any year, just not in my class. But the Rosenblatt mantra echoed throughout my body: "Teaching is a moral activity." Letting the error go was immoral and unethical, and *I knew that!* My pride was restraining me as was my fear of revealing my limitations. I learned the importance of being moral and responsible from the way I was brought up as a child. My parents taught me right from wrong, good from bad. So I struggled over how I would revisit the lesson without looking like a fool during my first year of teaching.

All night I worried about how I would revisit the lesson without focusing on the fact that I made an error. My sleep escaped me during that long, pensive night. I didn't want to lose my students' respect because of this grammar error. But I knew that I would lose self-respect if I did not face the challenge of correcting the error. My main fear was that Lou was in that class and knew more than I. But Lou's kindness toward me enhanced my admiration for him and for his grammar knowledge. Even at his young age, he knew that what I did was difficult yet necessary. He allowed me to grow in the wisdom of truth.

He gave me the chance to do what was right.

The next day came quickly. Walking into that seventh period English class, I said: "After dating your notebook for today's class, please go back to yesterday's notes and look at the singular possessive case. Change the apostrophe from the right of the *s* to the left of the *s*. Now go to the plural possessive case notes and change the apostrophe's place from the left of the *s* to the right of the *s*." I proceeded to re-teach the irregular nouns and the possessive case rules for them.

The stress and struggle from the night before faded. The students made the corrections, and we continued with new information. My *perfect* grammar background (or so I thought) needed improvement, and this was humbling. From that moment I embraced the importance of course content and methodology, but most of all of being human; and gaining wisdom from this experience enabled me to recognize the beauty of those students like Lou in my classroom.

Years later, Lou wrote:

> I remember the discipline, so important for young people. Without you, the rest will be a waste of time. You put the fear of God in most of us, and as in Proverbs and elsewhere, the fear of the Lord is the beginning of wisdom.

> —Lou, Facebook, December 24, 2011

Life Lesson Learned

I became stronger after making the decision to re-teach the grammar lesson, allowing the students to see my frailties. After that I began to love who I was—a person who could be humble and not a person who would hide in the falsehood of the greatest cardinal sin: pride. I learned that moving away from pride allows us to grow toward wisdom.

For this life lesson, I thank you, Lou.

CHAPTER 8

Never Judge a Book
by Its Cover

Mary Grace's Story

It was a few years into my high school teaching when I first met Mary Grace. She was a quiet girl who sat in my freshman English class, never giving me any problems. Being the youngest in her family whose siblings had passed through my classes and had graduated by the time she arrived as a freshman, Mary Grace was extremely timid and reserved—at least around me. What I remember about Mary Grace was that her eyes were crystal-clear puddles that illuminated the goodness of her soul.

I never had any trouble with Mary Grace. Always prompt for class, always responsible for her homework assignments, always answering the question when asked, and ready for whatever I asked were her traits. She was the youngest of four, shadowed by her siblings—until that one afternoon.

The teaching day was over, and I was preparing to leave my classroom. As I emerged into the hallway, there stood Mary Grace. She was timidly standing there, waiting for me to recognize her.

I did.

Meeting her with a smile, I asked her how she was and if she wanted anything. It was unusual for her to assert herself. She just remained silent every day in the classroom, doing her work diligently.

That day was different.

"What can I do for you, Mary Grace?"

"I just wanted to ask you how you stay so happy all of the time. I have never seen you in a bad mood or troubled by anything. Life seems so good for you, and I need to know what you do."

I looked at her eyes and knew that she was serious. Although I had several years of teaching experience at this point, paralysis stepped in, immobilizing me momentarily. This was not in the textbooks, yet I was responsible for this student. I took a deep breath and knew that this young woman was desperate to know the "password" and to have the keys that I possessed— her guarantee for a happy and peaceful life.

There was one problem—I didn't have the password. I didn't even know it.

I remember looking at Mary Grace, telling her that what she saw wasn't always reality, that the "book cover" wasn't always truth. Asking her to walk back into the classroom, I proceeded to tell her that the timing of her question was situational irony. At that point in my life, I was going through some professional issues that gave me moments of fear, questioning, and distress. (During that time I was struggling with my own professional questions: should I continue to teach in this school, or should I look for a position elsewhere?) The revelation of my turmoil surprised my student. Mary Grace was looking at a woman who did not have life harnessed as Mary Grace had suspected.

I assured Mary Grace that my persona reflected what she saw in order to keep the classroom a place of learning, a place for the students. My intent was not to bring my own problems into the classroom or into my students' lives.

And I never did.

As Mary Grace walked out of the classroom, I reached for my briefcase, left the classroom, and watched her fade around the corner toward the stairs that voiced the footsteps of thousands of students for so many years.

The year ended, and Mary Grace never met me again. She came to class, and she remained as diligent as she was before, always prompt for class, always responsible for her homework assignments, always answering the question when asked, and ready for whatever I proposed.

She never returned after school to my classroom after that one afternoon.

Her appearance was the same. Her eyes still revealed her soul's goodness throughout whatever unrest and discord she was experiencing, as I continued to work out my own struggles. Perhaps she found the password she was seeking.

Without a doubt, I could have used that password myself that year.

Life Lesson Learned

I learned to be more perceptive with my students. Students don't come into the classroom *tabula rasa* (like blank blackboards). They bring with them experiences, happiness, pain, sadness, challenges, pressures, confidence, no confidence, false confidence—so much that we don't see or have time to see. I found out that I represent more to my students than just one who shares knowledge about a subject. I share knowledge about life. And in this sharing, I must always remain truthful to each student and to myself. Sharing life with a student is healing. I hope that it was for her. I know that it was healing for me.

For this life lesson, I thank you, Mary Grace.

CHAPTER 9

D'Jeet?

Marco's Story

While I was teaching at the high school after several years, a young Italian man walked into my freshman English class with a wide and genuine smile perfectly positioned on his face. He was new to the class and new to the country, having recently emigrated from Italy. Marco had just introduced himself to a new world, one that held curiosity, new friends, and a new language. Without a doubt, this student was eager to learn and ready to settle into a new life. In class he listened, answered when he knew the answers, and had the English vocabulary to communicate those answers. But the important point about Marco was that he was unafraid to ask questions, even if it meant that he would linger after school or come into my classroom during his lunch break.

Wherever he went, he carried his Italian-American, American-Italian dictionary with him.

One afternoon when the class was at lunch and I was working in my classroom, Marco walked in to ask me a question.

His raven-colored, curly hair and bright, dancing eyes ignited the room with light and laughter. Simply stated, he was a joy to have in class, a young man who made an impression.

"Mrs. Sunyoger, may I aska you a question?"

"Yes, Marco."

"What doesa *d'jeet* mean?"

I vividly remember standing behind my desk with a handful of papers. "What, Marco?" I thought he was being facetious.

"What doesa *d'jeet* mean?"

When he asked me a second time, I knew he was quite serious, but I just didn't have an answer.

I asked if he had checked his dictionary for any word that was closely associated with that vocabulary. He didn't know where to begin (and I should have known that before I even asked). Yes, even I was stumped and had no idea what the vocabulary meant.

Four years of undergraduate general studies in English and (at that time) a Master's Degree in Modern American Literature abandoned me. My knowledge of vocabulary (I thought) was solid and rather vast, but I had never heard of that word before this.

D'jeet. D'jeet. D'jeet. I just did not know.

Suddenly I thought of something. "Marco, who asks you this word, and where are you asked this?"

"The studentsa aska me thisa every day. They saya, 'Hey, Marco, d'jeet?'"

I was baffled yet pursued the point. "When they ask you this question, where are you?"

"I sitta in the cafeteria during luncha, and the students comea over and say, 'Hey, Marco. D'jeet?'"

Then I knew. I solved Marco's mystery concerning part of the English language that had no meaning for this student. I looked into those deep, inquisitive, energetic eyes. "Marco, the students are asking you, 'Did you eat?' They want to know if you finished your lunch."

"Whatta?" Then he understood.

Speaking each word more slowly gave Marco the meaning to what was previously so enigmatic.

His new world suddenly became friendlier and more understandable. No, the students weren't trying to bully him or laugh at him. They just wanted to know if he had finished his lunch so that he could spend time with them.

As he walked out of my classroom, I realized how I had taken the pace of the English language for granted and how non-native speakers hear our words so differently than we do. His question made me smile, and I was so grateful that I had asked him a couple of specific questions that helped us solve the mystery of language. At that point we both learned some new vocabulary.

Life Lesson Learned

Marco taught me a great deal that day. He helped me recognize that we are different, seeing and hearing others differently. Students don't bring the same background into the classroom. My repertoire of knowledge expanded that day. There was no methodology text that prepared me for that specific moment. It was the dancing eyes and contagiously bubbling personality of a young, non-native speaking student who wanted so desperately to understand his new classmates. We want to belong to a community; but when we don't understand the language of that community, we become excluded from that community.

Marco was not embarrassed to ask for help so that he could become part of his American classmates' community. I learned never to be afraid to seek answers—that's how we learn. That's who we are.

For this life lesson, I thank you, Marco.

CHAPTER 10

Needles and Pins

JoAnna's Story

I finally settled into the profession of teaching a year and a half after I began. One day while driving the familiar path to the high school, I suddenly realized that I was not breathing heavily, and my heart had a normal beat. Prior to that time, I perspired and hyperventilated, my heart pounding hard, fast, and furiously. Poe's "Tall-Tale Heart" came to mind every morning as I parked my vehicle in the faculty parking lot. Every afternoon during the short drive home, I prayed that the Lord would remove the fear, that I would be myself, and that I would enjoy the classroom without the inner feeling of fright.

One day it happened: I no longer felt the extreme anxiety and terror that followed me throughout the first three semesters. My prayers were answered, and I was thankful.

During that second year while teaching American literature to my afternoon junior English class with an enjoyable discussion ensuing, I noticed JoAnna.

She sat in the middle row, middle seat. I knew JoAnna before she took my class. She and her family were not strangers. JoAnna sang in the children's choir for the church where I played the organ and where I directed the children's choir for Christmas every year. No, JoAnna and her parents were not strangers. They were consistent church-goers whom I saw every Sunday. The students liked JoAnna. Throughout the year, she expressed kindness to everyone, and everyone reciprocated. Her personality was sterling, yet she never became prideful with that gift.

In the classroom, JoAnna always had her hand up, her flashing white teeth concealing the answer that begged to be audible. She was Italian, and the ethnicity of that culture was evident in everything she did. With hand raised high, she exhibited some impatience if I did not call on her immediately. At times she would drop her hand in exhaustion (or despair), since others in the classroom needed their moment to contribute to class discussions.

She knew I had to call on everyone, but she sometimes forgot that.

One afternoon in the midst of discussing Pearl Buck's *The Good Earth*, JoAnna raised her hand…and raised her hand…and raised her hand. She never put her hand down. As other students raised their hands for classroom discussion of the literary work, JoAnna kept her hand elevated higher than the others, although she was unlike Horshak (a main character from *Welcome Back, Kotter*, a television show popular in the 1970s) with her intensity. She remained calm—yet persistent.

I walked up and down the rows, continuing with the discussion, calling on those students whose hands were raised first, not calling on JoAnna immediately.

Suddenly, JoAnna looked up and, meeting my eyes with hers, she waved her hand in a come-over-here movement for me to walk closer to her desk.

She had something to say and needed to say it *now*.

I walked toward her as another student was discussing the text.

"Mrs. Sunyoger, your skirt has a tear in the back."

"*Whhaatt?*"

"Your skirt has a tear straight up the back."

I knew that walking up and down the rows, as I always did, was not going to occur that day. Instead, I stood with my back against the blackboard for the rest of that period. I can't remember how much time of that class remained that day. But whatever the time was, it was endless…

I don't remember anything else we discussed concerning Pearl Buck's work, but I do remember that skirt. It was a brown pencil skirt—a tight one. A very tight one, apparently.

Facing the class for the rest of the period and waiting endlessly for the bell to ring, I proceeded to the home economics classroom on the first floor and looked for the teacher. Mrs. G. was preparing for her next class.

"Would you please sew the seam in the back of my skirt before the next class? I have a tear in it."

Mrs. G. placed me in her dressing room and immediately took the skirt to her sewing machine. It took a few seconds before it was finished. Standing with my back to a blackboard all day would be extremely demanding, since I was used to walking between the students' desks while teaching. Although I was a more seasoned teacher at this point, standing still with a torn skirt still bothered me.

In the dressing room, peeking through the curtain that exposed my body from the knees to the floor, I graciously waited, grateful that JoAnna was so persistent in alerting me to the tear.

I finished my teaching day, thinking that the students in that class knew what had happened and were quietly poking fun at me. Yet I felt as if I managed to escape humiliation, since a student took the time to inform me about more than a literary point. Instead, it was my torn skirt. I never had an incident like that happen again, although many other incidents have filled my professional days. And with those, I have become flexible. And with each new incident, I smile.

Life Lesson Learned

I learned that laughing with the students—even if the laugh is on me—is not that bad. Those moments remind me that I am human and have weaknesses that, when exposed, help me move away from pride to humility. With humility comes strength and membership into the human condition. Perfection is not available to anyone on this earth, and defeat lurks in the shadows when the challenge of trying to be perfect exists. We learn from our imperfections; this is what is important in life. I learned something priceless that day.

For this life lesson, I thank you, JoAnna.

CHAPTER 11

Life Happens

Alice's Story

Out of every pore of her skin shot electricity. When God created Alice, He found the largest electrical outlet and plugged her into it. Her light filled the room with a smile brighter than the Cheshire Cat's smile in *Alice in Wonderland*. As she walked down the high school hallway on her way to my English class, Alice led the way with her friends flanking her every step.

She was the queen.

Having Alice in class was enjoyable and delightful. She unknowingly drew the rest of the students into whatever conversation penetrated the room. Her bubbling personality, snapping eyes, wide and genuine smile, and pleasant demeanor captivated those around her.

She was someone anyone wanted to know and befriend.

One morning in English class, Alice was quiet, extremely quiet. Her typical personality of energy and spark was not a member of the classroom environment that day.

I noticed the difference and wondered why.

Before my class, Alice had Home Economics. There never seemed to be a problem. She was always on time, never missed a class, and turned in her assignments on time. Her contributions to class discussions were always welcomed, both by her classmates and by me. She was respected for who she was and for what she was—a truly good person.

But that day was different. *She* was different.

I asked my questions, waiting for Alice's hand to match her classmates' soaring hands. But that did not happen.

After my classes that day, I found out from one of my students that Alice had to be taken to the local hospital that was five or ten minutes from the high school. She had swallowed a straight pin while she was sewing in her Home Economics class.

Alice never complained that day in my class. She never said a word. That's what was different. She never discussed the short story or engaged in questioning the literary work. Alice came to class so that she would not miss the class notes and the class discussion. But she was unable to engage in the literary discussion—because of the straight pin.

That day for Alice was spent in the hospital going through x-rays that revealed a straight pin in her stomach.

Several days passed before Alice returned to my English class. When she returned, she again filled the room with her electric personality.

Life Lesson Learned

Alice taught me that teachers need to be more observant and should know their students well enough to see if something is wrong. Each student brings to the class a unique character and personality. When that character and personality are missing, the teacher must act. The teacher needs to ask questions, and if the asking interferes with classroom routine, that doesn't matter. What counts is finding out what is wrong with the individual and helping that person. I learned to respond to my students as people who need attention to matters other than academic ones.

Alice taught me to appreciate the beauty of each person and to protect that person's beauty.

For this life lesson, I thank you, Alice.

CHAPTER 12

This is For Looks Only

My Seventh-Period English Class's Story

I always wanted a beautiful, unabridged dictionary for my desk, one with an old, ornamental look that would be noticed and quite respected. When I was an undergraduate, having visited one of my professors in her office for some information concerning class, I noticed *the* dictionary on her desk. The book sat so stately, so proudly, so palpably perched above the other smaller books surrounding this professor's family of books. That dictionary left an imprint, an image I never forgot.

After my undergraduate years, I visited a small bookstore housing used books, searching for a dictionary comparable to the one I had seen in my former professor's office. Fumbling with shelves and shelves of books, I saw one waiting for me, waiting for me to adopt and to take it to a new home—my desk in my classroom.

My seventh period English class was the last class of the day. The students were high school freshmen who were really a group of enjoyable students. A small portion of Friday's classes (approximately fifteen to twenty minutes) was devoted to quiet reading. I approved the books selected by the students by supplying a reading list with the option of "first come first served" with the reading books listed.

I always looked forward to Fridays; and as I reflect on those days, I am certain that most of those students did also. We were quiet—and read. That's how we said good-bye to the school day; that's how we said good-bye to the academic week.

Just as the students engaged in the reading activity, I, too, brought my book and read at my desk. Modeling was always the focus of my education courses when I was working on my secondary certification (the term used back then but now referred to as licensure), so I emulated my philosophy and modeled for my students. Plus, I just enjoyed having a few moments to read my favorite literary works.

During that reading time, we all participated in the same activity—although separately. Perhaps that time enhanced the appreciation for reading for some of the students.

The situation almost seemed perfect, but one glitch remained. I can remember looking at my dictionary that perched proudly on my desk, admiring its ornate binder, its cover, its authority, its prestige. But I also remember that I never—*ever*—used it in class, whether I was reading or teaching. The treasure of language and its mysteries just sat.

I was afraid to use it in front of the class. For some reason, using the dictionary would reveal gaps in my "perfection." I was supposed to know all of those words. I was the teacher whom students depended on to teach them what they didn't know. So I *never* referred to it. I was supposed to know everything!

On those Fridays when I read a word that was unfamiliar, I skipped over it, wishing that I could call on my companion for information. I underlined the words so that I could go back later, when no students were watching, and search for the definition and reread those passages.

Somehow this did not seem honest, moral, and professional. It definitely did not exhibit good modeling. How could students model after this false *perfection*?

One afternoon, I fought with my internal conflict that I was conscious of while reading my literary text. Underlining the vocabulary words and yearning to use my dictionary became overbearing. With some hesitancy, I rose from my chair and walked around my desk, approaching the site of my dictionary. I reached for the book and turned from the undisturbed open page to the page that housed my vocabulary word. I found the word's definition. This was freeing. I had transcended the pretention of being perfect and performed the task that I had wanted to do for such a long time.

After that, students began to walk up to my desk and use the unabridged dictionary for their vocabulary words. I would sit and read, aware of students coming toward my desk, standing in front of the dictionary, and turning the pages until they found their answers.

I was never reluctant to use the dictionary after that first time. And to this day, I reflect on that fear that held me back. My desire to be perfect or to look perfect evaporated that day. I thank God that it did.

Years later when I started teaching at the university, the former professor I mentioned in this chapter was retiring. A few days before she left, she gave me her dictionary and its wooden, ornamental stand for my desk. I still have it.

And I use it.

Life Lesson Learned

My seventh period English class taught me a lesson, a most important lesson. These students created a risk-free environment for me to face my fear and challenged me to rise above the desire to look perfect, to appear to know everything, to be false and artificial in the classroom. Instead, I revealed my human side of not knowing every word in the dictionary and transcended the sin of pride by using such a valuable tool. When I did this, my students began to do the same by using the dictionary—one by one. We grew, one by one. But we also grew together. And from this, I learned to love my self and all of my imperfections.

For this life lesson, I thank you, seventh period English class.

CHAPTER 13

A Christmas Story

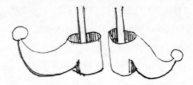

Leonard's Story

The Christmas report became a tradition in my classes—in all of my freshman classes. The first time I gave the assignment was during my first year of teaching. I asked students to do a small report covering Christmas traditions, unique celebrations of Christmas around the world, and symbols of the season. They could select any area they wanted. This offered the opportunity for students to break away from the usual assignment topics and to learn more about the Christmas season through this small report.

But the assignment became more elaborate every year.

For the first year, I asked the students to look for information concerning traditions of Christmas and how different countries and cultures celebrated Christmas, or for symbols of Christmas, or for Christmas myths (like La Befana in Italy). The report contained several pages with a cover page and could house pictures. As the assignment expanded, students wrote more elaborate reports containing more pictures and more interesting information. Students even wrote their reports, alternating the pages with red and green ink. Then the students started to write with red and green ink, alternating different paragraphs. Some students alternated every other word; some alternated every other letter. (Can you imagine how long that writing process would have taken? There were no PCs back then for these students. They wrote by hand.)

Every year I learned so much about Christmas. Having attending Catholic schools all of my life and teaching in a Catholic high school at that time, I wanted to complement the religious Christmas story by offering the students other topics that would also be interesting to read and to write.

As the Christmas project grew and continued to become more refined, the report partnered with a presentation that involved script, costumes, and dialogue. There were so many approaches to the presentation of the report, and students did their best in sharing their information from simply summarizing their findings and reading them to dramatizing them.

They were different and demanded so much work and energy, both in the writing and in the delivery.

I did enjoy watching these performances, finding that students took this opportunity to reveal who they really were as their personalities emerged in the presentations and in what they could really do.

From all of the performances, however, one stands out that I shall never forget.

Leonard did a report on the American Santa Claus's helper: the elf. His report was written in red and green ink and contained pictures that complemented his work. The day that he presented was quite a shock.

Leonard was a quiet boy. He was well liked, but he was very quiet in class and never raised his hand to answer a question unless I called on him. When I did focus on him for an answer, he knew the answer and was never hesitant to respond when I called his name.

But Leonard was always behind the scenes—until the day of his presentation.

Unlike the other students, Leonard started his presentation from outside in the hallway. When he walked into the room, the entire class gasped. There was at first silence; then there was an outburst of laughter. Leonard walked into the class with green opaque tights and a red elf costume. He wore a green felt triangular hat with a red ball perched on the top, and his feet were covered with pointed cloth shoes with white cotton balls bouncing from the tops of the toe area.

He really looked like Santa's elf. In fact, he acted like Santa's elf as he walked from side to side in front of his peers and in front of me. His report's information meticulously flowed from his lips from consistent rehearsal, and his delivery was flawless.

That presentation was a most enjoyable one, one that not only impressed his classmates but one that truly impressed me. We learned many details about Santa's elves that day, enjoying every piece of information from the elf in front of the classroom.

Life Lesson Learned

I recognized that individuals really do need those moments where they can shine and leave their mark when given the opportunity to share their God-given talent. When doing so, everyone involved gets a pleasant surprise. I learned that if we give others the chance to be themselves, we appreciate their talents, we learn—and we remember. Then we can, in return, share them with others.

For this life lesson, I thank you, Leonard.

Chapter 14

Five Seconds or...

LeAnn's Story

I knew that I loved grammar. This area of English is the mathematical, logical component that demands the attention of the left side of the brain, unlike the brain's right side, where literary interpretation resides. Even as a first-year teacher, I knew that grammar would be the most demanding subject matter to teach. Therefore, I had to work on a methodology that high school freshmen would enjoy.

That's when I created a method that worked—and that the students enjoyed.

Part of the grammar covered was the forms of *be*, the linking verbs, and the helping verbs. I asked the students if they could memorize these verbs and know them so well that they could say all of them in five seconds or less. At the time, I taught several freshman English classes and challenged all the students to this task. Every day for a few minutes, we practiced the verbs as I called on student volunteers. From memory, they said, "Forms of *be*: be, being, been, am, are, is, was, were. Linking verbs: be (all forms of *be*), become, grow, seem, appear, look, remain, stay, feel, smell, taste, and sound. Helping verbs: have, has, had, may, might, must, do, did, does, should, would, could, shall, will, can, be (all forms of *be*)" in front of the class. Of course, we did not concentrate on the time element, since we merely concentrated on the major categories of these verbs.

We repeated and repeated. As the great Greek rhetoricians taught so many years ago, repetition is the road to success for memorization: associate, focus, and repeat.

Students had fun. This was a challenge, a game. But they were learning a grammar game. We proceeded to the next challenge: the time.

I had my second-hand watch and timed each student.

After a few weeks, the contest began. Every student from each class had a turn repeating the verbs, trying to reach the five-second criterion. Students began with twenty seconds, fifteen seconds, ten seconds, and finally five seconds. The contest, I thought, was over until a freshman, LeAnn, stood up and took her turn.

LeAnn was a confident, smart, energetic student with an electrifying personality. She took a deep breath, pushed back her shoulders, and in a clear voice embraced the challenge set before her:

"Be, being, been, am, are, is, was, were. Be, become, grow, seem, appear, look, remain, stay, feel, smell, taste, sound. Have, has, had, may, might, must, do, did, does, should, would, could, shall, will, can, be."

There was no stuttering, no faltering, no hesitating, no abating in confidence. LeAnn enunciated clearly—

and that was also key—enunciated clearly each verb. She had mastered the assignment. But most importantly, she had fun with her challenge. LeAnn smiled in her calm demeanor with laughter in her eyes and a snap in her voice.

She did it!

She not only met the challenge, but she also surpassed the five-second criterion. After checking my second-hand watch, I realized that she said all the verbs—clearly—in three seconds.

Three seconds!

Suddenly, those verbs became the freshman classes' *Guinness World Book of Records* mantra—and LeAnn was the queen of saying them in record time!

Throughout that year and many years afterward, the "LeAnn's Three-Seconds Record" became the unbeatable record. No one ever said the verbs in three seconds; in fact, no one ever came close to it. Several students met the original five-seconds criterion, but no one ever broke—or even met—the three-seconds record. And throughout it all, we had fun, and students recognized those verbs and their functions.

The activity became memorable and bonded the classes into a community.

To this day, when I see my former students from those years of the five-seconds challenge, I hear the mantra begin, sometimes ending, sometimes skipping some verbs, sometimes complete—but never matching LeAnn's three seconds from so many years ago.

I have never seen LeAnn since, but I am certain that she has become a legend in those students' minds, as she is in mine.

Secretly, I have tried to meet or beat the LeAnn record. But I cannot.

Parroting is not a good practice for learning, and this I know. But the exercise was exciting, enjoyable, and engaging. Whether the verbs became useful for those students or not, I'll never know. But I do know that it created a community, and I do know that the activity has become a legend.

LeAnn remains a legend.

Life Lesson Learned

I found that taking risks with classes and introducing fun into a lesson surprisingly offers life-long memories. Looking at activities in a creative way does work when given a chance. My students had fun. I had fun. Being unafraid to break out of the box of methodology taught me that I could be myself and not worry about presenting that impersonal persona to the class. Feeling secure in my own skin has become the cornerstone to my life both in and out of the classroom. We should never underestimate what others can do and what we can do. The opportunity has to be given; that's all.

For this life lesson, I thank you, LeAnn.

CHAPTER 15

I Have a Secure Future

Jack's Story

Jack was a senior in high school, taking my Gothic Literature class as a requirement for graduation. He was tall and sported a strong physique, a quiet smile, warm brown eyes, and a respectful attitude.

But Jack just did not engage in any activity that went on in class. He was a loner, both in his school work and in his life.

One day after class, I stopped Jack before he left. I wanted to know if I could do anything to help him become more vocal in class and more involved in class discussions.

He looked at me and said with determination, enunciating each and every syllable, "I do not need this class or any class. My father has a job waiting for me at the steel mill. I'll start sweeping floors, making more money than you probably make now. It's guaranteed."

He was probably correct about making more money than I, but that wasn't the point. There were no guarantees in life, but I didn't know how to convince him.

"Use this time to your benefit, Jack. You may change your mind, or the job may not be there for you after graduation."

"Oh, it will."

As he walked out, I heard his response echo in my mind: *Oh, it will.* I still hear his words and see the secure look in his eyes, wishing then and now that life were that predictable.

He finished the course with me that year, graduated, and received the job at the local steel mill.

Years, many years, passed. One day I walked into a restaurant lounge. A man opened the door for me, greeting me. Suddenly he called me by my surname. As I turned to face him, I saw the strong physique, the quiet smile, the warm, brown eyes, and the respectful attitude.

"Jack?"

"How did you remember my name after all of these years?"

I just did. I remember your name because I'll never forget the certainty and secure statement you made about the job at the steel mill guaranteed by your father.

"What are you doing here?"

"I've been a bouncer for a few years."

A bouncer? Does he remember what he said to me years ago? Do I ask him about his steel mill position? What happened, Jack? Did the sure-fire guarantees in life backfire? What happened?

No words escaped. I simply thanked him for holding the door, told him I wished him luck, and proceeded into the building.

I never saw Jack again,

I wonder where he is today.

There is no local steel mill like the "old days" anymore. No secure jobs are waiting for young high school graduates.

Many men have been laid off or have been offered early retirement.

I wonder what the steel mill offered Jack.

Life Lesson Learned

We must never rest secure in what someone promises our future to be. We cannot depend on others or outside sources. We must invest ourselves and not depend on others, doing nothing and expecting "handouts." We must work during the here and now; we cannot lose the daily opportunities to grow and prepare for our life challenges. I learned never to be passive in this life. The Lord created us to act in a moral and positive way for others. To achieve this, we must do our best in the situations in which He has placed us. We must make a difference.

For this life lesson, I thank you, Jack.

CHAPTER 16

If I Ever Have a Son, I Hope He's Like You

Michael's Story

I met Michael during my first few years of my teaching profession. Our first meeting was in a high school freshman English class where Michael sat in the middle of the room, center aisle, a tower of youth. He was a quiet young man with a thin frame, yet as desirous to learn as he was tall. Michael was quiet, the quiet that recalls the quote, "You could hear a pin drop," but his answers were always partnered with a smile. His writing was good; he followed directions, explored the literature with intensity, and edited his work with precision and continued practice. He incorporated what I suggested and what others offered in collaboration concerning his writing. He was one of those students whose entire action foretold that he would accomplish his life's goals.

Michael was kind to his classmates who gave him their respect in return. His peers looked up to him for what he was, for who he was, and for what he did. Yet he did nothing for personal gain; his actions were intended for the goodness of others.

There were times when Michael stood aside for others to leave class before him; there were times when he opened the door for his peers and for me. There were times when he gave a kind word to someone who was having a hard day. The young man was simply tuned into the human condition, a gift that very few have at this young age.

One day after school, I was working in my classroom when Michael walked in, asking if he could talk with me for a little while. I told him that it was fine and that he could have a seat. He began telling me about his family and his brother who had died from cancer. His story narrated the love that he had for his mother and his recognition of her strength and faith in God after she had lost her first son. For this, he wanted to do something special for her on her approaching birthday.

He bought her a ring and wanted to bring it to school to show me, asking if I thought that she would like the gift.

"Michael, whatever the ring looks like, it is from you—your mother's son. She will love whatever you give her. Even if you give her nothing, your love is all she wants. That's the greatest gift."

"But I worked so hard all summer, cutting grass and doing odd jobs so that I could save the money to get her a beautiful ring. I want to do this for her."

Love filled his eyes, his smile, and his soul. I knew it. I could feel it. So I told him to bring in the ring and that I would look at it.

A few days later, Michael came into my classroom after school.

He carefully extended his closed hand, housing a small box. He opened his hand as if he were unwrapping a bandage protecting a small child's wound; he lifted the box's lid. It was a box from a local, well-known jewelry store. I recognized the name. Inside was a square emerald stone surrounded by small diamonds couched in a cushion of yellow gold. This exquisite gift was juxtaposed by the young age of the giver. The receiver was a mother who was cherished, adored, and loved by her son for her selfless acts of love.

Your mother will tell you to take the ring back to the store, Michael. She will tell you that the ring is too expensive and to save the money you worked so hard for all summer. Her heart will swell with love for what you did, yet her mind will help her refuse such an extravagant gift, I thought.

"The ring is absolutely beautiful, Michael. You love your mother very much and recognize her love and daily sacrifices she makes for her family. Not too many young men would see this at your age." I looked into his eyes that were seeking affirmation for this act. He received it.

"If I ever have a son, I hope he's like you."

I really meant what I told him, for having a son who loves a mother so much is a blessing, a blessing that must be appreciated. If I would have a son someday, I wanted that kind of love from him, a son who respected my sacrifices and a son who was grateful for what his parents did for him. No, it wasn't the gift of a ring; it was the gift of love.

His smile met mine as he gently closed the ring box.

He walked out of my room that day, and I never knew any more about his mother's gift.

But it was not for me to know. I was warmed by the thought that Michael included me in one of the greatest acts of love in his life.

And I prayed to God that night to bless me with a son who would love me as much as Michael loved his mother.

God did.

Life Lesson Learned

Sometimes we think that an expensive gift reflects how much another person means to us. Michael's gift for his mother was not the emerald ring; it was the labor for the money that he earned for the ring; it was the time he took to select the perfect birthday gift; it was the love and respect he had for his mother. Love is what is priceless…not material objects.

As members of the human condition, we contribute to the beauty and goodness in the world through our selfless acts of love. We should "love our neighbors just the way we love ourselves." The expression of love this young man reflected that day is the love we all should share. Through Michael, I learned I want to give selflessly to others, in both my professional life and personal life.

For this life lesson, I thank you, Michael.

CHAPTER 17

You May Talk 'O Gin an' Beer...

Another English Class's Story

The freshmen loved the literature from the anthology in my high school freshman English class. Teaching literature was exciting, engaging, and entertaining. I, in turn, loved working with the community of readers as we discovered what was between the lines of these short stories. Analysis was daunting, at times, but when we moved into the poetry section, the challenge seemed insurmountable. The boys in the class were alienated immediately, and the girls were somewhat reluctant to swap the stories for the poems.

But poetry was part of the curriculum, and the poems were waiting to be read, analyzed, and discussed.

Every year I struggled with introducing the genre of poetry. We brought in lyrics from current songs; we looked at jingles and lyrics from television commercials, and we perused the textbook. That's where the interest and the interaction fizzled. The textbook's poems were one-dimensional in print, and the students were "somewhere else" when I asked them for the interpretations.

Because I did not want to duplicate another boring beginning of the poetry unit, I decided to have students really become engaged with the literary works by using as many senses as they could, besides the sense of sight.

So we began the poetry unit with working on reading the poems aloud—with enthusiasm, enunciation, and excitement. One poem I chose was Rudyard Kipling's "Gunga Din." Not only did the students have to read the poem, but they had to read it with a British accent (since Kipling was British). I had my tape recorder in front of the class. Not only did the students have to read the poem one by one, but they also listened to their dramatic reading after they finished recording.

Every student had the opportunity to practice, to read, and to record. Each one stood by the recorder as the entire class listened. After everyone read and recorded, we listened to the voices on tape.

Gunga Din

You may talk 'o gin an' beer
When your quartered safe out here,
And you're sent to penny-fight and Aldershot it,
But when it comes to slaughter,
You will do your work on water,
And you'll lick the bloomin' boots o' them that's got it.
Now in Injia's sunny clime,
Where I used to spend my time,

A-servin' of 'Er Majesty the Queen...
Rudyard Kipling [iv]

Students blushed, laughed, sighed, shuddered, and smiled. The tone was set. The students forgot that they were afraid of poetry due to their absence of understanding this genre; they were just having fun. The poems were read, analyzed, and discussed. And we became a community of readers—a community that appreciated the beauty of the word and the expressions of feelings through poetry.

My students became engaged and excited that day. And to this day, I am certain that some of those individuals in that freshman class remember what we did when poetry was introduced—and some may remember with a smile, the way I remember that day. The strategy was a gamble, but the technique worked.

I have always loved poetry; and when I find it daunting to teach, I simply ask each student to extend one hand so that—hand in hand—we can begin the journey that poetry offers. Together the journey is traveled, explored, and experienced. From that, those travelers will look more deeply into life, into others, and into self. The soul-changing experience waits for us in those poetic words of beauty.

Throughout that exercise in poetry, I think my students embarked on a journey and received poetry's gift—the universal truths of life.

Life Lesson Learned

Not only does it take courage to explore different ways to do something in life, but it also takes courage to actually do them. I learned to trust others so that I could try something new. I learned to believe in others and to believe in myself. Without a doubt, the "routine" can be safe—but boring. When this is the situation, we have to break out and simply be creative.

My class taught me to laugh, to create, and to share the beauty and goodness of poetic expressions with one another. When this occurs, we become better, more spiritual, more caring for each other, and more enlightened. We see some areas of life that we simply could not previously see. Poetry reveals this to us…if we only listen.

For this life lesson, I thank you, freshman class.

CHAPTER 18

It's Hard to be King

Bishop J. King's Story

I really enjoyed being the high school English department chair. My responsibilities required not only teaching English classes, but they also comprised many additional organizational duties, such as book ordering, working with my English faculty, making decisions concerning issues that emerged throughout the year, among so many others. One of my biggest responsibilities was evaluating the members of the English department, both the full-time members and the part-time members.

One part-time member of the department was the bishop of the Catholic diocese. He was a kind man, an intelligent man, a good soul, a good shepherd, and one who loved the arts and the language. When we needed a teacher for a freshman English class until we could hire someone, he volunteered to teach the spring semester.

Spring semester moved quickly, and I knew that soon I would begin the annual evaluation process of the English teachers. Saving the bishop for last—*how could I evaluate the bishop?*—I prayed that the evaluation would never materialize.

But it did!

Room 222 was the first room on the high school's second floor that met anyone walking up the main stairs. Yes, the room was still there, waiting for the occupants of its seats and the teacher who would acknowledge his place in the room. The teacher of this class was the bishop.

I positioned myself in the back of the room, sitting in the last seat against the door. No one was in the room when I selected my spot. Being there for a matter of moments, I soon found that I was no longer alone. Students entered, marking their spots with their backpacks. As soon as everyone was seated, the bishop entered through the door located at the front of the room. He took the podium with respect and humility. He respected his students, and he reflected humility. Yet he was the Bishop, the shepherd of thousands of Catholics in the diocese as well as the teacher of those students.

So I sat, watching, listening, and writing—writing ideas concerning the bishop's knowledge of the subject and his methodology in teaching it.

I—sitting in Room 222 with the bishop, the shepherd, and the teacher—had to observe and evaluate this great and humble man.

After class, I wrote the evaluation, knowing that I had to meet with the bishop in order to discuss

the positive and negative areas of his teaching that I witnessed that day. This was the evaluation process for all department chairs with their department faculty.

But this was the bishop, and I had to meet this great and humble man.

So the date was set, and we met, and I was nervous.

The bishop listened to what I had to say with a calm and welcoming demeanor. Typical to his personality, he was quiet, with eyes full of wisdom, permitting me to speak.

My anxiety lasted only minutes, for his soft eyes, engaging smile, and willingness to articulate his ideas concerning education and pedagogy relaxed me. Yet the humility was always present. He never used his powerful role as the bishop during that conference; instead, he was an English teacher who simply wanted to do his best for his students and who wanted to learn what he could do to improve his teaching.

This was *his* evaluation; but as I reflected on that day, I truly thought that it was *mine*.

The bishop allowed me to perform my duty as the department chair throughout his evaluation, knowing that I was growing as a professional. I was so fearful of evaluating him; yet in his wisdom and humility, he made me relax throughout this experience where I grew in wisdom. Being "the king" of the English department was hard, but the true king was the man blessed by God who sat before me, in wisdom, grace, and humility.

Life Lesson Learned

I was a young teacher when I journeyed through that experience as the chair of the high school English department. Yes, I was frightened to discuss with him his teaching at first; but throughout the years, I have recognized the blessings I received by evaluating the bishop of my Catholic diocese. His wisdom penetrated my very being, yet I was so nervous that I did not initially recognize this. He modeled for me that no one is above learning how to improve. There are times when we think that we are above that. But we must be humble and not prideful, no matter what our position may be. The bishop taught me humility, acknowledging every situation as a blessing and learning from each. He taught me that loving means being humble, being thankful, being kind, and being an individual and not just being a title or position. The bishop taught me that I could do what I never thought I would do. Through his wisdom and humility, he left with me a memory that I shall cherish forever. *Requiescat in pace.*

For this life lesson, I thank you, Bishop.

CHAPTER 19

If You Only Knew

An Unnamed Student's Story

For ten years I taught English from freshmen to seniors. The eleventh year was quite different.

When I received a phone call from a two-year institution, I accepted the adjunct position in the department of English. To start, I was teaching a freshman composition class and a technical writing class. The chair of the department decided on the text and on the syllabus (a list of assignments for the course for the entire semester), so I had no control over what textbook I would use.

Preparing for the courses, I remember calling the secretary, asking where the textbooks were.

"Don't worry. They'll be in your mailbox here in the office on the Monday morning before your first class."

"What? But I need the class textbooks before that day!"

"Why?"

Why? She wants to know! What good is getting the textbooks a few hours before my classes! I want to review them and plan the term for the students in those classes.

Then I realized that some individuals think that those who teach don't need to prepare: teachers just know all that is needed to know. I deduced that from the secretary's comment.

"Don't you already know your subject? Don't you just look over the book before the class?"

"I really need the textbooks so that I will be prepared for the classes. That's all."

A few days later, I found my textbooks in the mailbox and thanked the secretary.

All summer I fretted, somewhat fearful of my change of my professional context. No longer was I a teacher in a high school English classroom; instead, I taught in a higher education setting. This was both exciting and frightening.

But I was ready to accept the challenge.

Or so I thought!

The day came, and I felt the way I did during my first year of high school teaching.

I drove to campus with my textbooks and syllabi. My heart pounded. The restroom was close to my classroom, so I went in to gather some composure. While I was in the stall working on my breathing and nervousness, I heard the voices and chatter of excited students who were preparing for their future.

So was I.

Between the noise from my nervously heavy breathing and my preoccupation with the "what if" situations that might occur during my classes, I heard—above the rest—a frightened voice filtering through the door.

"I am so scared! This is my first time ever I have been on a college campus. I am so scared."

She continued to talk about how afraid she was—how afraid.

I then peered through the stall door and saw a young woman standing with her back to the sinks and mirror. Her friend was standing between her and me.

My composure was returning—a little, but I was still nervous. I knew that this girl had as much fear—if not more—as I did (and I was the professor!).

"You'll be fine. Just give school a chance. After today you'll fit right into the academic schedule and won't even remember worrying and fretting over your classes. This is just the first day."

This is just the first day!

I heard the words of her friend and let them sink into my being. The walls of fear and panic began to crumble, piece by piece. I emerged from the stall and looked at the girl whose eyes were clouded by confusion.

"Listen to your friend. But it's fine to be a little nervous. This is new, untraveled territory. Soon you won't think twice about this new chapter in your life. It's normal to be nervous. And, besides, you're not the only one who is nervous about a new beginning. I am really nervous, and I am the teacher!"

I'll never forget the look on her face when I revealed my secret. Her eyes were like a drain in the bathroom sink with the rubber stopper removed as the water slowly runs down and out of sight. Instead of fear, her eyes were filled with surprise. The young student was suddenly more relaxed. She wished me luck as I wished her the same.

She left, never turning around. As I watched her leave with her friend, I knew that she would work her way through the experience and would tackle the challenges of higher education and of life's challenges.

I wonder where she is today.

Life Lesson Learned

I found that when I think I am alone with my problems, my fears, and my unsettled life (at times), I am not alone if I let others know. Being a member of the human condition requires that we recognize others and have compassion for them. Students are individuals with fear and trepidation; teachers must be aware of that. Revealing my weakness helped another person, and it helped me transcend my trepidation and to grow.

For this life lesson, I thank you, unnamed student.

Chapter 20

A Creative Imagination

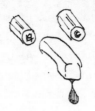

Fred's Story

With teaching come the excuses—the eternal and typical commonplaces that teachers hear. Some are the following clichés: "I lost my homework," "My dog ate my homework," and "I left my homework at home." Some are more original: "The bath water overflowed and ruined my homework that I was reviewing," "My grandmother moved before I could go back to retrieve my homework," and "The hard drive crashed."

Besides the homework excuses, some late-for-class excuses also echo: "The car broke down," "I was stuck in traffic," "My ride never showed up," and "The electricity turned off sometime during the night."

But very little compares to two of the greatest excuses of all time.

While teaching the eight o'clock Advanced Composition II course every Monday, Wednesday, and Friday at the university, I met an unforgettable, quite creative student. Fred was an excellent writer—when he decided to tackle the assignments and turn in the work. Naturally, I wanted him to succeed—not simply in writing but in the values that come with living (i.e., accepting the responsibility of choices).

My university course guidelines are quite clear and simple. Every semester, I introduce the students to these guidelines so that there will be no equivocal areas concerning the outcomes of not following these points. "If you are late for class three times, I will ask you to withdraw unless there is a reasonable excuse. Tardiness is a reflection of disrespect for the professor, for the other students in the class, for the course, and for you."

Fred was quite consistent and predictable with his tardiness. Several times he walked into the classroom, disrupting the students sitting closest to the seat he selected. The noise drew my attention from the lecture notes to his entrance. One day, I finally asked Fred to withdraw from the course after several verbal warnings. Fred was shocked, surprised, looking like a fallen warrior. Inviting him to my office, I listened to his excuses that reflected such a creative imagination.

"The first time I was late for your class was because of the traffic. I was stuck and couldn't get to campus on time." (This is one of those "stock" excuses.) "The second time I was late for your class was because my mother didn't get me up on time." (He was twenty-one years old at the time!) "The third time I was late was because while I was taking a shower, the caulking around the tub became loose. Before I knew it, the water ended up all over the floor, going under the bathroom door and into the bedroom. I had to clean everything and ended up being late for class."

That was inventive, some possible dialogue for a narrative. But I didn't believe it. I still don't. So many times I've wanted to ask his mother (when I see her in my hometown) if she "failed to wake her son on time," or if she "had a water problem" those days Fred was late for class. I also taught her and her siblings when I taught for ten years in high school, so I wouldn't feel uncomfortable asking her about these excuses.

But I don't.

I asked Fred to withdraw and to take my course another time when he was ready for it and its responsibilities. I reinforced that he was an excellent writer—with a vivid imagination.

He withdrew, although he never re-registered for the course; instead, he changed his English writing concentration major, and I never saw him again.

Reflecting on the action that I took is still the same: I knew that I had to be consistent and uphold my guidelines. Other students in that class were on time. Any other action on my part would not have been fair to either those students or to Fred.

Waking up every morning takes courage, and walking into a classroom demands fortitude and passion. Teachers make decisions every day, and we pray that they are the right ones. There is no text that can be tabbed with the perfect answers to every problem.

Each situation is unique. However, we don't realize that when we are working through our own education and studying the content and the methodology.

My university students in the Teaching Writing as a Process course frequently asked me—and still ask me—why the authors of the textbooks offer theory and the implementation of that theory without addressing those I-dare-you-to-teach-me students. How do we teach them well?

How do we know if we are touching hearts and not piercing those hearts?

Life Lesson Learned

Fred taught me that I cannot believe every excuse, although I cannot be a complete skeptic either. Telling students up front that they need to have a good track record is what counts at the end of the day (or at the end of the term). We need to stand up for those students who have accepted the responsibility of work and studies, yet we must *never* hold any grudges toward other students. Besides, Fred reminded me that students really do have creative imaginations!

For this life lesson, I thank you, Fred.

CHAPTER 21

I Don't Do
8:00 a.m. Classes

William's Story

William was one of my university students, an English Writing Concentration major who was a fine writer—when he wanted to do his work. He always had a smile on his face, seemed to be well-liked by his classmates, and knew what good writing is. He crafted it well.

The advanced writing course was a required course for all English writing majors, so there was no way that students working through their program of study could avoid this class—not even William. There was nothing wrong with the class (according to William), except its time. It was offered only at 8:00 a.m. on Monday, Wednesday, and Friday. The positive side was that it was offered every semester; the negative side was that it was offered only at 8:00 a.m. on Monday, Wednesday, and Friday.

The first time William walked into the class, he was alert, energetic, and extremely engaged in the discussion of literature and the various authors' writing styles. He enjoyed the artistic craft of writing and explored this through his participation and questions. The writing he did was refined, controlled, and inventive. I enjoyed reading his papers.

In addition to the classroom discussions covering the essays we read, there were papers to write, a metacognitive letter for each paper (a written exploration and connection with past papers, with authors' writings that students emulate, and with the process that the students use for the particular paper), and a heuristic (strengths and weaknesses that students continue to be aware of while editing). William did what the syllabus disclosed and did it better than so many others in the class.

Yet as the classes continued throughout the semester and as the papers grew, William began to wilt. There were class days where William was nowhere to be seen. Not only was he invisible, but so were his energetic participation and contribution to class disscussion. His peers began to recognize the absences.

Incredibly, the number of absences almost balanced the number of classes he attended. By the end of the term, his attendance determined his grade. But the grade in no way reflected what his talent was as a writer. Class attendance counted, and that was one criterion that he had not met.

One day I asked William what happened. In T.S. Eliot's words, William had "started out with a bang" and ended "with a whimper." [v]

William met me at my office on campus, trying to find the right explanation that would work miracles. He presented his argument that he had the ability to write a variety of genres and could write them well. I agreed. He recounted his literary perception to analyze, discuss, and contribute new ideas to classroom discussions. I agreed. But one key criterion was class attendance, and that's what he did not meet.

There is little opportunity to grow as a writer if an individual does not read, analyze, discuss, or incorporate writing techniques into his or her own work. William did not do any of these as the semester moved along. The other students did.

As we continued with our conversation in the office, I asked William what he could do to get to the early class, besides waking up. I asked him what held him back from being able to make it to class.

William suddenly looked at me and blurted out, "I really don't do 8:00 a.m. classes! I never did like to get up early for class."

"What are you planning to do after graduation?"

"I am going to teach high school English."

"William, what time do you think schools start?" were the only words I could think of asking.

I remember looking at him. His smile flashed genuine peace, yet he was clueless concerning the time that every school I know starts in the morning—early. And I prayed that night for him, because he was given a gift of writing and revealing beauty and truth through words, yet William refused to use his gift. He simply buried his talent, rebuking one of the greatest moral lessons taught in Timothy's *Parable of the Talents*. [vi]

And I prayed that he would share those gifts someday, that he would spark students into loving literature and writing, and that he would meet the first criterion of this profession: to be on time for class.

Life Lesson Learned

William taught me that it is so important to know our talents, our gifts, and our passions, along with our deficiencies. What we do throughout life must reflect who we are and what we are capable of doing. Our talents must be compatible, or we won't be productive in helping those around us. This hinders us from bringing out the goodness of others if we have trouble knowing ourselves. No matter what, we must recognize the truth concerning who we are, what we are, and what we can do. Our talents—these gifts from God—must not be buried.

For this life lesson, I thank you, William.

CHAPTER 22

More Than an Assignment

Rachael's Story

Rachael was a non-traditional student who sat in the last seat in the first row. At first, I thought she chose that seat because of her height. She was much taller than the other students and could possibly block the view of those sitting behind her. Years later, I discovered from Rachael that she chose that seat because she was scared, scared to be in a university setting after so many years had passed since her high school experience. But she had made a decision to continue her education. So she came to campus. My English composition class was her introduction into university academic life. And, again, she was fearful about taking the first steps of this new journey.

After listening to the course syllabus, the guidelines, the assignments, the responsibilities, the expectations of the course, Rachael told me—years later—that she had cried while driving home. And home was several miles away from campus. She almost did not come back.

But she did. And I'm glad that she made that decision.

For every assignment, Rachael worked hard. Her first paper was stilted, exploring the writing strategies and experimenting with her writing style. The next assignment revealed a little more flexibility in her writing where her voice was beginning to emerge. It was a humorous yet sensitive signature—her mark as a writer—that would enable her to create resounding stories later in the course.

As we progressed throughout the semester, I presented the one assignment that focused on purpose and audience, two key components of writing. Each student worked on a creative short story that reflected a theme—death. This concept had to be explained to a seven-year-old.

Rachael wrote a short story—"Home Run"—with a seven-year-old baseball player (the protagonist) whose father was killed in an automobile accident on the way to the baseball field where he planned to watch his son play. When he is told about his father's death, the young boy's depression causes him to quit playing baseball, since he feels that it is his fault that caused his father's accident. Max's coach visits him and explains the death of the father in a metaphor. He tells Max that God knew that Max's father was a good baseball player, so He now wants the father on His team in heaven. God calls the father home to play baseball, and God is the umpire.

The creative work met the criteria of purpose and audience; in addition, Rachael assumed the male persona, giving the text added dimension, along with a deep pathos in the narrative.

Her paper etched into the hearts of the readers (my university writing majors and me).

I knew that Rachael had this emotion and talent in her soul, even though she did not believe that she could achieve this in her writing. She worked hard, probably through many tears and revisions.

But she did the assignment and *did it well.*

Rachael and I still send notes, e-mails, words of encouragement, and updates about both of our professional and personal lives. So it was many years later that one day Rachael told me about the dilemma, her struggle, with the "death paper." Immediately before she started back to school at the university, Rachael was working through chemo and radiation treatments for breast cancer.

She was dealing with death—the avoidance of it—in her own way, and writing the paper was very hard for her. She explained years later that she did not want to face death by writing about it at first; but as she wrote, the process became a discovery, a discovery of self—her self. This process became one of healing.

Rachael persevered. To this day when I present writing sessions and/or teach purpose and audience to my classes, I use Rachael's eight-page short story—

small yet powerful—so that my students may realize that they, too, have the ability to craft a memorable piece.

Perhaps my students will gain more from the activity than simply doing just another assignment. Perhaps their compassion for one another and for life will become deeper. Perhaps they will realize how priceless the gift of life is.

And, yes, Rachael is a survivor!

Life Lesson Learned

Rachael taught me about the depth of writing and its purpose. She taught me about perseverance and persistence. Rachael modeled hope, faith in God, and faith in herself. Rachael taught me the meaning of humanity and the purpose of writing about it. I learned to dig deeper beneath the one-dimensional lines in textbooks and on students' papers.

For this life lesson, I thank you, Rachael.

CHAPTER 23

Fear of Failure

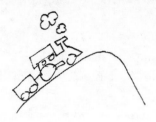

Judith's Story

I love school! I have always loved school, being in a classroom and learning all that I can. Reading expands my world and deepens my love for the human condition, and writing allows me the avenue to share my thoughts with everyone. When I was young, I couldn't figure out how I could stay in school and not be noticed as I aged.

Then one day the idea whispered the answer in my ear.

Being a teacher would allow me to be in a classroom and age without notice, for teachers do age as perennial youth presents itself every year on the faces of their students.

Teaching university advanced composition courses and business and professional writing courses (among other writing and literature courses) was most enjoyable. Every semester I met new and excited writers and readers who (on the whole) wanted to learn and to grow as writers. Judith was one of these students. She had the same goals as the other students to develop her writing ability in the business and professional writing course, but she was a non-traditional student who was several years older than the traditional university men and women.

That first day in my class, Judith sat in the first seat, second row. She had a look of excitement and the desire to learn stamped on each eye—attentive to every word that I spoke. As the classes continued throughout the semester, Judith worked hard and long, turning in assignments that reflected careful work and rigorous hours of revising. She moderately engaged in class discussions, deepening the insight from class discussions because of her life experiences in the army, in the business world, and simply—in life.

Students looked up to Judith and respected her presence in class. The classroom was Judith's family, and it showed in her demeanor. The involvement in class discussions was a comfortable holy spot for Judith.

Until the midterm exam.

This was the first time in over thirty years that Judith sat in a testing context. The midterm looming ahead was worse than facing a fraternity "hell night." She was paralyzed the day of the exam from her self-imposed fear of failure.

And that's just what happened—she failed the midterm exam.

As I returned the infamous blue books (exam books for midterms and finals where students write their answers), I watched her face turn as white as snow and the color in her face melt as quickly as snow on a hotplate. She robotically left the class when it was over and proceeded—somewhere.

Later that day, Judith knocked on my office door, asking if she could speak with me for a moment. I asked her to sit down and waited for her to begin the conversation, knowing that it would focus on the midterm grade. Instead, she held out her hand with a form—a withdrawal slip—asking if I would sign it so that she could officially drop the class. Her breathing was like a racehorse desperately working its way to the finish line, but I wouldn't allow the race to end. The paper shivered as she reached out her hand toward mine.

"Why are you dropping the course, Judith?"

"I failed the midterm exam and don't think that I can do well in this class. I started college so late in life. Maybe I'm not college material. I thought I was at some point."

"Why are you talking like this when you have enjoyed the class, contributed to class discussions, engaged in the assignments, helped others with their questions, and never missed a class? What is shackling you and holding you back from your dream of receiving a university degree?"

"I'm afraid. It's been years since I was in a classroom. It's hard for me to remember what I study. And…I just don't want to fail."

Her fear of failure was dominating her choices in life. She was prepared to give up and to quit.

"I am not going to sign your withdrawal slip, Judith, because I know that you have what it takes to forge ahead and to reach your goals. You can do this if you transcend that fear that is restraining you."

She looked puzzled yet relieved. As she left my office with that blank withdrawal ship in her hand, I knew that this was the right decision.

It was!

Judith finished that course many years ago; in fact, she finished her undergraduate years receiving a degree from the university. In addition, Judith continued her education, receiving an M.A. degree. She then went to China to teach English as a second language. In addition to the teaching and traveling, Judith wrote many textbooks.

Judith is my friend, but she first started out as my student. I thank God every time I hear from Judith about her additional endeavors, and I smile.

She faced her fear of failure and transformed into the Judith she wanted to become. She became the Judith whose potential I saw sitting in that classroom so many years ago.

The Jewish heroine with the name Judith who conquered the Assyrians was the Christian woman in my class who conquered her self-imposed enemy—her fear.

When Judith and I e-mail one another or call one another, there are times when the conversation of the F midterm grade surfaces.

And we chuckle.

Life Lesson Learned

Judith taught me to face my fears, to challenge myself, and to conquer whatever is restraining me. This process may be somewhat daunting, but having a good support group and working with a positive attitude are the tools needed for success. But most of all, Judith taught me to be faithful, to have a strong faith in God, and to turn over what bothers me to our Lord. Her belief in the Lord and her trust in Him enabled her to move forward. Her faithfulness to her goals and her love for Christ gave her the wings she used to soar to the heights of her accomplishments. Judith reinforced my own faith.

For this life lesson, I thank you, Judith.

CHAPTER 24

Never Say Never

Bridgette's Story

For years I wanted to develop a writing course that would connect the Department of English with the Department of Education. After teaching for a short time at the university, I finally succeeded in creating a course designed to teach Education Language Arts majors the methodology of teaching composition.

This course was an exciting one, since the fear that many future teachers have is knowing what good writing is but not knowing how to teach students written discourse—and how to teach it well. When I advised my own English majors who were working on their licensure to teach, I reminded them that this course was one required by the state (Ohio). The English majors who were not working on a teaching licensure had the option to take the course, using it as one of the electives available to them in their program of study for the English writing concentration degree. The class, therefore, comprised both types of students.

Bridgette was one of my best writers as an English writing concentration major. While taking the Advanced Composition II course, Bridgette wrote persuasive papers with meticulous research, using a writing style that was controlled and mature. She knew the craft and developed as an effective writer over the four years in my classes.

One semester when Bridgette came into my office for advice concerning her schedule, I suggested that she should take the methodology class in case she ever decided to work on her licensure.

"I never considered being a teacher, and I won't ever go into Education."

"Why? You are a gifted writer and could offer students whom you teach so much insight concerning the written word. Why haven't you considered going into the profession?"

"I just never thought about it and don't want to think about it as an option."

Why wouldn't she want to share her talent, her gift with others? She was personable, knew her content area, worked well with others in the classroom (as evidenced when she engaged in collaborative settings in small groups), and looked very comfortable in the classroom. Her presentations were prepared, smooth, and interesting with memorable delivery. Being so compatible with content and pedagogy, why would she be so adamant?

I asked Bridgette to take the course and to experience the environment of learning about methodology for a semester. If she still had no desire to teach, the course would still be a vital stepping-stone to her B.A. degree, since it fulfilled the electives requirement for the writing concentration.

Bridgette refused and registered for another writing course, claiming that she would never want to teach English.

Until that day during her senior year.

I was sitting in my office, grading papers (as I always do), and Bridgette knocked on the door, asking if she could talk with me for a few moments.

"Come in, Bridgette."

She was a tall woman and appeared serious—without the personable and smiling appearance she brought into the classroom and into my office other times.

"Have a seat, Bridgette."

I knew. I knew that there was some struggle going on inside of her.

"What's bothering you, Bridgette?"

"I am preparing to graduate this year and have been struggling with something. As I continue to discern what I want to do with my professional life, I keep going back to the idea of teaching. There is passion when I think about being in the classroom and helping other students learn and develop. But I don't have any methodology courses, especially methodology courses in teaching composition."

It took some time, but she found her calling: sharing her talent of written discourse with others.

"What could I do to try to catch up?"

I remember explaining that the Master's degree in Education would be the next logical step if she wanted to take that journey.

She did.

For some time I hadn't seen Bridgette after her undergraduate graduation. Then one day Bridgette walked into my classroom. For her Master's program she took my course that was offered in the summer. It was a small class in the seminar room on the first floor. As I took my seat at the head of the oblong table, Bridgette walked into the room. She proceeded to the chair on my left, being the first one on the left side of the long, wooden table. I looked at her; she smiled at me.

Without saying a word, we both knew she was in the right place and would truly enjoy the path she selected.

That summer session was a good one with hard-working students with meaningful and insightful discussions, making connections between the theory of written discourse and its methodology. Although those connections were necessary and important, the connections made between student-and-student and student-and-professor were the valuable and priceless ones that deepened our lives.

There are times when I think of Bridgette, especially when I think that I am certain that I don't need to engage in an experience "not suited" for me.

Before meeting Bridgette, I missed out on skiing, horseback riding, and writing this book. Those were experiences that I rejected.

But not anymore!

Life Lesson Learned

I learned that I need to keep myself open to positive experiences that emerge in my life and to other areas of growth and learning. Being attentive to a recurring thought, to a consistent tug in one direction, makes a difference. "Never say never" became a reality for me, and over the years—those many years since Bridgette returned to my classroom—I know that all things are possible in God, and I am open to the goodness He brings into my life.

For this life lesson, I thank you, Bridgette.

Chapter 25

Never Assume

Lena's Story

Writing Creative Nonfiction was one of the classes I designed while teaching at the university. It represented a new genre of writing and attracted some of the best English writing concentration majors.

When the semester began, I saw faces of doubt, fear, and gloom sitting before me in the classroom. Every face looked like that. Any glimmer of hope and of life was buried somewhere down deep, with an optimism of doing well wrapped in a cloak of confusion since this new genre was foreign to the students taking the course.

After lectures explaining the genre and exhibiting models of this type of writing, I witnessed the curiosity overshadow the confusion while offering students the opportunity to write their own works, employing the characteristics and rules of this genre.

The journey was a new one, a strange one yet an exciting one for the students. They permitted me to lead them into this unknown land, giving them the tools to explore the area with my encouragement and their excitement. Some of the topics for the assignments covered hair loss of women who struggled with cancer, wedding gowns passed down from generation to generation, horse training for Dressage, the loss of a mother, conversion, the death of a father, a brother-sister relationship strengthened through the game of Lego, the insight into who one is and what one can do through the metaphor of the game of chess, the rite of passage from childhood into adulthood through the metaphor of the bumblebee, and so many more creative and quite interesting paper topics.

The papers were a joy to read, and I read every one.

I remember Lena, an English major who enjoyed writing and working in a collaborative environment in the classroom. Her contributions to class discussions and to other students in a one-on-one relationship enhanced the growth of those working with her.

Lena was a pleasure to teach: she had a sunshine smile, fire-streaked hair, and a delicate laugh. Being blessed with these attributes, Lena also loved literature and writing. She was quiet, meek, humble, and responsible. Yet she was smart, dependable, and trustworthy.

For this class students engaged in collaboration where they worked with other students. During this phase of the writing process, we discussed the characteristics of this "fourth genre" and referred to the models of literature we read and analyzed for the class.

In addition, students volunteered to read their drafts for comments and suggestions from both the students and from me.

"Every writer is a reader, but every reader is not a writer."

I still hear that sentence echo in my mind from my own graduate classes. It just made sense.

The day arrived when the papers were edited enough to be read to the class. The students were several drafts toward the final piece and wanted some feedback while editing before turning in the final paper. Consequently, the papers were ready to be shared. Several students volunteered. Some did not.

Lena was one of the students who did not volunteer.

She sat in the first seat, second row, always engaging in whatever I requested. Being a fine writer, Lena *had* to be a reader (or so I thought). That's what I had learned in my own graduate studies.

So I called on Lena to give her a chance to receive some feedback for her work.

Being attentive and disciplined, Lena responded when I asked her to read.

She read.

When she began to read, the words came out slowly, without rhythm, and not in their natural word groups. For example, instead of reading "in the middle of the lake," Lena read: "In the…middle of…the lake." Reading her paper was laborious and long, but Lena read. She read several pages that seemed endless. What could have been a few minutes for "the read" turned into long, arduous, unconnected semantic noise—there was no meaning.

But Lena read.

Her reading did not seem to bother her. She didn't seem to listen to herself. But we listened, unable to understand the content through the interrupted flow of her words. But we still respectfully listened.

When the class ended, I promised myself that I would never force students to read by calling on them if they did not volunteer to do so. I would merely recognize those students whose hands were raised.

Before Lena, I never thought about calling on a student to read. I never thought about the sentence: "Every writer is a reader, but every reader is not a writer."

Life Lesson Learned

I learned that I must recognize the silence of another person and not force that person into an activity if that individual does not volunteer. What works for one person does not always work for another. Each student is different, unique, and I must remember to respect and to dignify the gifts of each person. Since that day I have never called on someone to read in class; instead, I merely ask if there is someone who would like to read a paper or part of a paper. For those who do not volunteer, I have learned to recognize and appreciate their individual gifts.

For this life lesson, I thank you, Lena.

CHAPTER 26

The Studies in Fiction Dead Poets' Society

Lori's Story

Lori was in my university Studies in Fiction class, and it was quite a large class. In fact, there were fifty-two students in that room. Lori was in her senior year, taking the course to fulfill the humanities core requirement for graduation. Being a Journalism major, she knew that her program of study did not allow for too many humanities courses. So that semester Lori registered for the fiction class.

I had known Lori for some time. She was a member of Theta Phi Alpha sorority, Alpha Zeta Chapter that I had joined years ago when I was a collegiate. Lori took some of my composition courses that fulfilled her journalism program. So I saw her frequently on campus throughout her four years.

Lori was intelligent, kind, extroverted, disciplined, and organized. Her ability as a writer was outstanding; her writing voice was strong and truthful—just like her. The papers she had written were pleasurable to read and to evaluate, containing controversial topics supported with solid research and an unbiased position with logic and meticulous prose. Having her in class was enjoyable: she challenged me and shared mature ideas with a professional style.

But this fiction course was different. The class read and discussed literary works written by a variety of authors. Emphasis on the analytical level was a major part of class discussions, but attention to the evaluative level of reading (how the story affects the lives of the readers) was a powerful aspect of the discussion.

Stories aren't meant to simply be analyzed; they must touch the soul of the reader. They change or help to change the lives of those who visit the work. A reader has an epiphany—an aesthetic, soul-changing experience—for having read the work, that is, a great literary work.

I said this to the class, and I believe this point. It comes from the center of my being. For years, I have been changed by great literary works I read. The Georges in this life (John Steinbeck's *Of Mice and Men*) reflect the struggle between what is right, what is wrong, and what is moral. An appreciation of having two good parents, unlike Francine, (Betty Smith's *A Tree Grows in Brooklyn*) helps me understand the rules they gave me to live by, and the importance of living a humble life

instead of a prideful life (Guy de Maupassant's "The Necklace") navigates my actions.

These were the stories we read, and there were many classes of good discussion with students engaging in serious dialogue as the semester progressed.

Throughout the discussions, Lori was one of the biggest contributors. Her insights ignited students, engaging them in mature, insightful, and solid analyses of the literary texts. The use of the primary sources supported Lori's comments concerning theme, characters, climax, etc. But her ability to make the stories connect with her own life was the moving force behind her reading and discussion. What she said gave students a model for the aesthetic reading that changed readers' lives. The class meetings raced quickly to the finish line that semester—without anyone noticing. We were a community of readers in that classroom. And we enjoyed it. But the semester soon ended.

The last time I saw Lori in my classroom was on the final exam day. Taking the exam with the other students, Lori sat in the second row from the window in the third seat from the front. Two hours were designated by the university for the final exam, so there was enough time to answer my four lengthy essay questions. As I monitored my exam and worked on grading other final exams from other classes, I felt some remorse that we would never be in that same context again: the same literature course, the same short stories, the same students, the same—the *exact* situation. This would never happen again. We had shared so much with one

another in this reading community, and we enjoyed so many stories with one another.

After the two hours passed, I collected the papers. Turning my back to the class as I reached for my briefcase, I again turned around, placing the papers in the case. Looking up, I saw Lori standing on the top of her desk: straight, at attention, quiet, reverent, and frozen. Suddenly, I heard from her lips:

"Captain, my Captain."

Immediately the other students rose, standing on their desks, repeating the same words. "Captain, my Captain."

Each student rose, one by one.

One by one.

"Captain, my Captain."

Frozen, I stared at Lori with tears in my eyes. I could not fathom what was happening. It seemed like a long moment in time, but it happened in an instant. Yet that instant will remain with me always.

We were a community. The stories changed our lives, and we became better individuals because of one another.

I can still see every student being a witness to that—especially Lori.

Life Lesson Learned

Lori taught me the importance of being honest, truthful, and reflective. In addition, she encouraged me to move away from the ancillaries that tell teachers what to do or how to teach a narrative and to truly help students transact with the literature. This changes lives. The stories become mirrors for readers to see themselves, to learn about themselves and about the human condition. I learned that there is more to teaching than the components and vocabulary of literary texts. For a semester the class became a community of readers, a family of readers, a family that cared about one another. We do touch lives, and we need to let others know that their presence on this earth and in our lives makes a difference—a blessed one.

For this life lesson, I thank you, Lori.

CHAPTER 27

Ignorance is Not Bliss

Rob's Story

He seemed quiet and extremely shy, one student in a class of fifty. Tall, thin, with eyes that held secrets, Rob sat toward the middle of the large classroom in the center row. He needed the literature course to fulfill his humanities core, being a science major as an undergraduate. Since the class was so large, Rob easily faded into the background of students' voices engaged in participation and discussion of the literary works. Therefore, I decided to have the students keep journals (I believe in the benefits of journaling—building confidence and the voice of a writer), writing their thoughts concerning each story they read for the class.

Even with such a large number of students, I still wanted to connect the literature with writing, so I required a journal of entries that each student had to write. Some of the entries were focused, and some of the entries were unfocused. Every story read required a page of comment concerning the literary work. Without a doubt, collecting these journals and reading each entry from the large class would be monumental, but my responsibility to my students demanded that I should spend time with each. I did not shirk the respect owed to each student, so I decided to collect the journals in the middle of the semester and again at the end of the term.

The term progressed with energetic discussion and eager questions about the stories. For every story there was a page of reflection from each student, waiting to be collected and read before the midterm exam.

As the students wrote, I asked them to work with a partner who would comment in the dialogue journal as needed.

Before the midterm exam, I collected the journals as I had stated on my syllabus at the beginning of the semester. Reading the journals was enjoyable, although, again, it was quite time consuming. But I did read the entries and commented on the students' thoughts. Yes, I did appreciate what students had to say and what students offered to their journal partners in their dialogue comments. I read with ease and enjoyment—until I came to Rob's partner's journal.

Kim was an extremely quiet student, especially in that class of fifty students. Easily lost in the numbers, Kim displayed attention and did her work, but she never discussed or offered any verbal insights into class discussions concerning the literary works. Yet she was a good student who received good grades on her carefully carried-out assignments.

When I opened her journal in order to read her reflections emanating from reading the narratives, I thought I would have a "good read."

Kim's ideas were solid, mature, sound, and insightful. The stories moved her into the realm of evaluating herself, her actions, her dreams, her accomplishments, and her own world. Yes, the narratives were aesthetically touching her soul, making her different from the Kim who walked into this class weeks ago.

As I continued reading her entries, I saw her partner Rob's written discourse commenting on her reflections. As I read through his words, I froze. Rob's comments overpowered Kim's insightful and soul-changing words. Her words of pure thoughts couldn't breathe under the constraints of the harsh and foul words from her partner, a partner in a journaling context where partners are supposed to trust one another with their reflections, where partners are in a safe place, a risk-free context where they do not have to worry about what they are saying. Yet as Rob's words overpowered the page, Kim's words died and shriveled. His abrasive comments concerning the female protagonists in the stories, his blasphemous sentences concerning the sequence of events of the stories, his outrageous disrespect for his journal partner spurred me to call Rob into my office for his withdrawal from the course.

First I thought long and hard; then, I asked him to come in to talk with me. In the meantime, I talked with Kim, telling her that she should have seen me as soon as the language and disrespectful imagery found in Rob's comments started. Kim was afraid to say anything and allowed Rob's behavior to continue. Reassuring her that this would never happen again, I asked Kim never to allow anyone to strip her of her God-given dignity and personhood.

Then I talked with Rob.

He came in, only because he had not received a grade for his journal and wondered why there was none given. With no hesitation, I told him that I would not allow him to dehumanize another in the class, that I did not appreciate his inappropriate attitude toward the course and its requirements, and that he was no longer a member of the reading community in that class.

In other words, I told him that he had to withdraw.

"I won't withdraw from this course! My dad is an ophthalmologist and has big plans for me, and I am not leaving! Besides, he is paying big bucks for this course!"

There was no remorse, no recognition for what he did or for how he had acted. There was no concern for Kim, for his classmates, or for me. There was only concern for him and his needs.

I remember sitting and staring at his shallow and ice-cold eyes. *For Kim and the others in that class, he needs to leave for this term and return when he is ready for this course.*

"You must withdraw."

"I'm not! I will be in class and will not withdraw. You can't make me!"

Never in my life have I ever said what I then did state, and never in my life have I repeated it.

"Then, Rob, if you insist on coming to class, I will not recognize you. I won't call on you. I won't read your journal entries at the end of the term, and you will no longer be Kim's partner—or anyone else's partner. And…if you want to know what your grade is for this class, I can give it to you today."

"It's just the middle of the term. How can you know my grade?"

"I know your grade, because it's an F. No matter what, the grade is an F. So you may come and sit in the class all you want, but you will not be a participant, not after your immature and disrespectful attitude toward your own classmates. You deserve nothing more than the F. When you are ready for this course, you may take the course another semester. But this semester is not an option for you."

The look on Rob's face was unforgettable. I still see those eyes full of confusion and discomfort. The feigned innocence was gone. His ignorance was suffocating; it choked the life out of a good woman and out of me. Yet his selfishness screamed the loudest.

I never saw Rob again. For the rest of the semester, I witnessed a woman develop in confidence and trust as she shared her thoughts with another journal partner for the second half of the term. And we both learned.

I pray that Rob learned, too.

Life Lesson Learned

I found that when an individual is too afraid to speak up when there is disrespect or inappropriate behavior by another, we must be the voice for that individual. We need to be alert and aware of what is going on around us with others in our lives and in our world. Sometimes we do not allot the necessary time for us to explore and inquire. Talking with Kim and asking Rob to leave my class was difficult, but the choice was necessary for fairness, justice, and concern for a healthy environment in the classroom for the community of readers, for a community of good people.

From this incident, I learned to be more explicit with the criteria for each course assignment. There is no room in life for ignorance, not the ignorance originating from "not knowing," but the ignorance originating from simply being selfish. Those around ignorant individuals experience an environment of discomfort and suffocation. This kind of atmosphere eradicates the God-given gift of being a human person with a voice. When an individual loses voice, we must stand up and speak up for the voiceless. We have no other choice. We must be strong and courageous.

For this life lesson, I thank you, Rob.

CHAPTER 28

Lizzy the Lizard and Theresa the Toad

Marie's Story

Marie was a tall woman with sparkling eyes; with dancing strands of soft, brown curls; with a gift for academic inquiry and challenges; and with a smile that invited anyone looking at her into a world of peace and joy. She was simply a good person. Being around Marie was rejuvenating and refreshing. She made those around her feel special, confident, and happy. Besides these gifts, Marie was a gifted writer. However, there was one major problem: she was a Spanish major and not an English writing concentration major. I wanted her in my major; she was that talented.

Marie was one of the students in my Advanced Composition II class. Meeting all of the writing requirements for the course, Marie proved again and again that she knew the process of writing, the craft of writing, and the beauty of sharing the word. For one assignment Marie wrote a short story about a little girl named Lizzy who is best friends with Theresa. With the narrative's setting being the Arizona desert, the girls are always outside, exploring the wonders of nature together. They are both seven years old with shared secrets, shared dreams, shared after-school walks and hikes, and even shared candy treats.

Every day after school, either Lizzy is at Theresa's house, or Theresa is at Lizzy's house. They are so close that they even name each other: *Lizzy the Lizard* and *Theresa the Toad*. These two young characters reflect the goodness of the human race in their relationship of friendship and love in Marie's short story. These two little girls reflect the beauty, goodness, and truth belonging to the human condition.

After a couple of days of not seeing Lizzy at school, Theresa becomes worried and concerned; so after school, Theresa goes to Lizzy's house, only to find her in bed—sick. Theresa does not know that her friend is dying from cancer.

Marie wrote this work for the class requirement of meeting the criteria of the audience and purpose of a narrative. Without a doubt, the short story met the challenge and met it well. Marie's paper contained pathos and ethos. Her imagery was superb, and the language was delicate and quite appropriate. The characters were genuine. The work was—and still is—memorable.

To this day, every time I teach a new class about the primary and secondary point of the narrative—purpose and audience—I refer to Marie's work and/or read it to the students. Inevitably, the students shed tears while

I have to stop periodically to dry my eyes and clear my voice.

I make it a habit of keeping the best papers on file, and this is one of my best papers.

For the entire semester, I tried to "convert" Marie from her desire to major in Spanish to my desire for her to major in English.

I never succeeded.

One day before the end of the term, Marie came to me, letting me know that she was leaving the university in order to pursue her love for Spanish, continuing with her major closer to home at the University of Arizona in Tucson.

I was crushed.

Not wanting to lose this opportunity to work with Marie in developing her as a writer and in reading more of her works, I explored the possibilities with her about her future if she would stay.

She was unwavering.

At the end of that year, Marie did leave and went back to Arizona and to her love of Spanish. I wonder where she is and how she is doing. I wonder if she has written additional narratives and has created more literary children who have touched the souls and lives of her readers. I wonder if she has continued to bless those around her with her insights, her compassion, and her contributions to the human condition through her craft.

I truly hope so.

What she gave me that semester will remain forever. In my own way, I share her words with others in order to give them an aesthetic, soul-changing experience.

In addition to offering to others a world of growth and aesthetic insight, Marie demonstrated that students are writers and can grow into becoming great writers.

So, wherever Marie is, I hope that she, too, remembers her "Lizzy the Lizard" and "Theresa the Toad." These two little girls who reflect goodness, beauty, and truth in mankind are memorable, as timeless as the great Gatsby, the great Hamlet, the great Oedipus, and the great protagonists from so many great literary works.

Life Lesson Learned

We have gifts to share and ideas to leave through language to others. Perhaps our names will not be carved next to the name of Shakespeare, Sophocles, Aristotle, Plato, St. Augustine, and so many more, but what we have thought and what we have to offer in our own ordinary way does make an extraordinary difference in the lives of others. From these two beautiful characters who represent innocence, love, affection, purity, and eternal loyalty, I have grown stronger and more compassionate in my attention to the human person. In addition, I have had a soul-changing experience.

For this life lesson, I thank you, Marie.

Chapter 29

Too Much Sun!

Sister and Katie's Story

Summer classes at the university are always smaller and more personal. The sessions go by so quickly, and the weather usually invites the enclosed classrooms to expand to the outdoors. So when it is nice outside, we usually walk to the courtyard, sitting at the picnic tables for that day's class. The literature class is so conducive for this kind of outdoor class; students discuss the narratives as they engage in themes, settings, characters, plots, conflicts, analyses, symbolism, and all the language that belongs to the study of fiction.

That one summer started out like any other summer with classrooms extending to the outdoors. There were no more than seven in the fiction class, so it was easy to find a spot in the courtyard and to have room at the picnic table for all of us.

Katie was one of the students in the Studies in Fiction class, as was Sister, a Carmelite nun from California who was working on her Education degree. Of course, being a religious meant wearing the appropriate habit of that order. Sister's was a full veil and brown habit. Seeing Sister in my class was not unusual, for there were many priests and religious taking classes on campus.

Sister was extremely quiet at first. But as the session continued, the small class size elicited more discussion from each student, including Sister. In the class with Sister was a young, red-haired woman with emerald eyes and porcelain skin. Katie was an extrovert who loved stories and the discussions emanating from literary works.

Every class session was exciting, engaging those few students into deep insights of the human condition of choice, morals, ethics, symbolism, relationships, truth, and the beauty of humanity. Comparisons and contrasts with other works arose as did agreements and disagreements with one another. But the class was congenial, respectful, and academically inquisitive. The community of readers developed immediately.

One day the archetypal question arose: "May we go outside for class today?"

Looking outside, I saw the sun, the cloudless sky, and heard the wind whispering, "It's a beautiful summer day. Come."

So we did.

I still remember the scene—university students with me sitting around the picnic table under the cloudless sky and hot sun. In fact, I had to get my sunglasses out of my vehicle: it was that bright.

We discussed; we engaged in a dialectic concerning the narratives; then, we left for the day. The community of readers would meet the next morning.

And that we did.

It was like the previous day. It was bright, sunny, with the wind whispering, "It's a beautiful summer day. Come."

After the prayer before class and before we began with the discussion of the literary work, I asked the students if they wanted, again, to have class in the courtyard, since we did not expect many more warm, summer days like the two recent ones. Looking at Katie, I was surprised at her extremely red face.

"What happened to your face, Katie? You have quite a sunburn!" There was no difference in color between her hair and her face.

She looked at me rather sheepishly. "I *did* get too much sun. My skin is so fair, and it's hard on my skin, sitting in direct sunlight."

"Knowing that, why would you want to sit in direct sunlight? Where were you?"

"I was with you sitting at the picnic table for three hours for class yesterday."

I remember her face, her eyes so full of truth and humility.

"I am so sorry, Katie. I wish you would have told me."

Then I looked at Sister, the religious in a full brown habit with her veil and with her quiet humility. "Sister, I am sure that you didn't enjoy the outside heat either yesterday."

"If we don't have to go outside, I would appreciate that," I heard Sister say.

I felt like an idiot that day. What was I thinking? Who did I think was in that class? Had I truly observed the students with whom I spent my life for three hours on a daily basis during a summer session?

I apparently did not.

Life Lesson Learned

I found that my comfort isn't necessarily a representation of all those around me. Sometimes, it is better to leave a location, a setting, a classroom environment alone. When life turns and twists a little, those around us may not feel comfortable enough to speak up. Perhaps the risk-free environment has not been created for the freedom of those individuals around us to voice what is on their minds. We can change situations; however, we must be alert, aware, observant, and courageous enough to create a risk-free environment for those around us. We are not the only ones in our world.

For this life lesson, I thank you, Sister and Katie.

CHAPTER 30

Tell Me What to Think!

Charles's Story

Charles was new to my university class. He was a Business major taking my Business and Professional Writing course in order to meet his requirement for the Business program of study. This was not unusual, since I taught many business majors, nursing majors, science majors, and others in this course. Some students in this class were my English majors, taking the class in order to meet their English program of study as one of the electives.

I met many university students from a variety of majors, students working toward becoming a member of their chosen community's profession. And that semester, I met Charles.

Every class meeting, Charles sat in the first seat in the first row by the windows—to my right. Every class meeting revealed his shyness, his seriousness, and his sensitivity. When called upon, Charles answered with hesitancy…but he answered. Confidence was the friend he needed. But she hadn't introduced herself to him yet.

The course went quickly that semester, and the students bonded into the community that I strive to develop in every class: family. But Charles kept his distance. He was "far back," too withdrawn from the class. But I did not have any complaints; he did his work, and he listened. I waited for him to become more comfortable and to add to class discussions. His voluntary participation would emerge, or so I hoped.

Midterm exams were approaching, and students were in their "zone" of preparation, with some visiting my office with questions. The scene was a familiar one, just like an old friend who visits me every semester at this time. So the dynamic of the occasion was nothing new.

Until I met Charles…

One afternoon after the Business and Professional Writing class, I was working in my office. Charles stood by the door, waiting for me to recognize him. With my door open, I saw him and asked him to come in and sit down. The look on his face revealed concern, confusion, and consternation.

He was angry.

Asking him why he was in the office, I tried to dodge the bullets as his eyes darted from the floor to his hands to me. With his eyes finally meeting mine, Charles punched the words with force.

"Why are you giving us a midterm exam? I have nothing in my notes for preparation. You needed to give us notes on handouts, on the board, on PowerPoint, notes I could copy in my own notebook and have in order to study for the exam. I don't have anything right now I can work with for a midterm! When we are in small groups, offering suggestions to one another about our papers, I become upset. These people are as stupid as I am. Why should I listen to them when they talk about my paper and think that they know more than I do? You are the one who should give suggestions—only you!"

Stupid...stupid...stupid.

That word still echoes and reverberates throughout my entire being. I'll never forget that afternoon and those words—and that look on this student's face.

My mind raced. Suddenly I was back in one of my own graduate classes as a student. The professor was discussing the types of students who pass through classes every year. One type of student mentioned is the "doing school" student, the person who needs notes, who needs handouts, who needs to be told what to study, what to do, what to learn, and what to "feed back" to the professor in a testing situation in order to achieve success. And in the classroom, success is an A for these students who never question any points given in class. The professor is the transmitter of knowledge in this transmission model of teaching, and students parrot what is said—without questions. Yes, these were the "doing-school" students. They know what to memorize for an exam, forgetting everything after it's over.

I remained calm, although deep inside I was a leopard, ready to jump toward my prey. But I waited,

composed myself, and with firmness in my voice and with an unwavering eye, I calmly began…

"Charles, this is a course where critical thinking is key, where class discussion enables students to enter into a dynamic of discussion and disagreement, of community collaboration, of respect for one another's knowledge represented through participation. This is the course's methodology. We will engage in this dynamic more and more throughout the semester. And the exam does not evaluate how much you have memorized and repeated. It evaluates your thought process in this subject area and your ability to communicate effectively and efficiently."

I continued to discuss the importance of respecting others and the various gifts that they bring to a group, of dignifying individuals, and of making decisions instead of doing what others say without thinking.

Charles walked out of the office that day disturbed, distraught, and disappointed with my response. He returned to the class and remained for the rest of the semester, but he did not join the class community.

He waited impatiently for the dynamic of the classroom to change; he waited impatiently for me to tell him what to think and what to say.

What he waited for never happened.

To this day, I wonder where Charles is and how he is doing. By now, I do hope that he has moved away from the "doing-school" model toward the critical thinking community where he can make his own decisions instead of doing what another says without Charles giving it thought. Perhaps he'll come to realize that thinking is necessary—not repetition without meaning.

Wherever Charles is today, I wish him well.

Life Lesson Learned

I saw another side of the human condition. Thinking that students appreciated one another's insights and knowledge, I was surprised to find that there are some in this world who really want to be told what to think and what to do so that they can succeed. As I look at life, I realize that questions engage individuals and help to clarify confusion. People are paying attention when they ask questions. There is great danger in being apathetic. No matter what, I learned that respect for another can never be abated or negotiated. We must dare to be courageous and confident enough to challenge, to think, to question, and to dignify another while we are seeking truth. In this process, we must respect one another, for God did not make us "stupid."

For this life lesson, I thank you, Charles.

CHAPTER 31

Sherrie and Shakespeare

Sherrie's Story

The university class was a good one. It was a big class, since it was a freshman course, but the energy was electric. I felt the shock every time I faced those eager eyes and flashing smiles. The fall semester moved quickly with the discussion of essays and editing papers. We were family as we encouraged one another with writing techniques, the between-the-lines information in literary models, and more effective editing strategies for the different writing discourses. Yes, the semester moved quickly, smoothly, and unforgettably. We offered suggestions to one another and listened to one another.

We cared.

In this class was a young woman interested in developing herself as a writer, as a thinker, as a contributor to the class community and to the world community with her own writing. Sherrie was an English writing concentration major and really enjoyed writing. Her writing was exceptional; her thought process and analysis was deep and mature. With the discussions in class, she offered information that made her listeners think, discuss, and grow.

Her eyes glistened and glowed every time I modeled another writing technique and another point about a literary work, techniques that help students craft their papers.

I assigned a variety of writing topics weekly. But one unforgettable class assignment was modeling writing strategies that we found in literary texts. The one strategy that I gave was a chiasmus—the strategy that offers an ornamental way of making a statement in a memorable way. The ancient Greek rhetoricians stated that memorable writing is in the style. Style is ornament, and this is what makes a point memorable.

Chiasmus was one of the writing strategies I shared with Sherrie's class that day. I gave the class examples. The famous Kennedy quote "Ask not what your country can do for you—ask what you can do for your country" [vii] ignited interest; the more unfamiliar Jessie Jackson line from his 1984 Democratic National Convention Address, "I was born in the slum, but the slum was not born in me" [viii] stirred curiosity. However, completing the trio of literary examples of the chiasmus was the powerful line from *Macbeth*: "Foul is fair and fair is foul." [ix] These are simply a few of the many examples found in literary works, speeches, and advertising. As I gave the examples, I asked the students to write their own and to include them in their writing.

Sherrie wrote one that I remember to this day.

"I cannot write Shakespeare, but Shakespeare cannot write me."

When she offered to read her chiasmus in class, we listened; I smiled. Yes, we cannot write Shakespeare: each one of us has a voice, a style, a distinct personality unlike any other. That's what makes this world so interesting, so challenging, so surprising. We are all different. The classics should not intimidate us; they offer the truth of the human condition along with aesthetic beauty and goodness.

Sherrie proved this with her chiasmus.

Years passed, but I never forgot the example—Sherrie's chiasmus.

One afternoon, I received a surprise telephone message from Sherrie. She had just taught her first university English composition class and thought of me. So she called my office, letting me know about her accomplishment. She wondered if I remembered her. I smiled, knowing all along that she and her chiasmus were remembered after all those years. Her chiasmus sustained the courage and strength that writers need. Her chiasmus reflected the craft and art of language—memorable language created with the use of powerful ornament.

Sherrie loved "the word." Her love for language and its ability to create beauty was evident then; her passion to share her love was quite contagious.

Passing down the passion for "the word," Sherrie found her place in front of her classroom; and there, she reveals the craft and art of language.

I wonder if she is still sharing that passion with others—with her own students in her own university classroom.

I wonder if Sherrie has her students writing a chiasmus.

Life Lesson Learned

Sherrie taught me that I cannot expect my students to write exactly like those great authors who have written time-tested works. The expectation is unfair. We need to give one another the opportunity to become who we are. And that is the goodness that we give to one another. Why should we want to be *exactly* like another when each one of us is so different? Yes, we need to learn from the greats, but we must insert ourselves into whatever it is we undertake.

God created us into His image and likeness, but He gave us our differences and our uniqueness. That's what we are blessed with and, in return, we appreciate one another for who we are; therefore, we courageously share our differences and learn from one another. Yes, we learn from Shakespeare and appreciate the beauty of his writing, yet we don't want to write exactly like him. We have a voice, a style, and no one can write like us—not even Shakespeare. So I learned to appreciate each student and each student's gift—the gift of self, of voice, of style, of beauty.

For this life lesson, I thank you, Sherrie.

Chapter 32

Thou Shalt Not Steal

Mark's Story

The class was large but not large enough to stop me from assigning a research paper as a requirement to complete the course. The university freshmen comprised the English composition class that wrote the term paper assigned during the spring semester every year. The course was strictly research, and the teaching was grueling at times. There was nothing I could do except teach the research process—a step-by-step approach for solid, academic research and its organizational structure. So many steps were important; however, there was one most important concern throughout the entire process: plagiarism. Strict emphasis was placed on plagiarism, since the university had a formal, written policy concerning the outcomes if someone were found plagiarizing. The faculty followed the regulations faithfully; I know I did. I was a staunch supporter for not stealing another's words, for not stealing anything.

One spring semester, I had a list of authors whom we were reading. Each student had to select for research an author from my handout and tell me his or her choice as soon as possible so that I could remove the author's name from the list. Some authors were Henry James, William Faulkner, F. Scott Fitzgerald, Ernest Hemingway, John Steinbeck, and James Joyce. They were all my favorites, but I never told the class whom I loved to read the most. I treated all the authors the same, and I respected each student's selection as if it were the only one on the list that was my favorite.

And with this disposition, I worked through the initial stages of the research process. One of the first research steps for the class was to go to the university library and find out where the reference books were kept, what they were, and what information was contained in them. Some students had never worked through the research process as carefully and as meticulously as research demands. Working through this research process involves full attention to avoid plagiarism. Consequently, the time in class commenting on plagiarism and my editing and revising with the students in order to avoid plagiarism was one of my course objectives.

Every semester I began the course by encouraging my students to remain attentive to plagiarism and to remember the risks involved in plagiarizing.

Every semester I closed the term by reminding the students to review their work for plagiarism. The students checked, edited, worried, reviewed, removed, and reworked throughout their research process.

I was alert to the possibility of plagiarism, but I couldn't conceive the idea that a student at this stage would plagiarize.

I was wrong!

I told my freshman class that I would spend time in the library researching texts if I noticed anything in their papers that was questionable—and I would spend time checking these areas carefully. What I did with the research writing class was to save the major paper until the last part of the semester so that by then I would know each student's writing style and could detect somewhat better the plagiarized excerpts, if I questioned some areas of a paper signaled by the change in writing styles.

In addition, each student wrote a metacognitive letter at the end of the research paper, indicating the process taken, the pitfalls, the revisions, suggestions from the collaborative sessions, and the class readings and models of other authors' styles that influenced the paper and its process. The student's style in the research paper and the student's style in the metacognitive letter should be the same. And if not, I pursue the process of checking for plagiarism. The metacognitive letter where students discuss their thoughts throughout the research/writing process is a "gatekeeping device" for me. There is where I detect their "true" voice.

That semester was no different. The students turned in the research paper with the metacognitive letter and waited for my evaluation. As I read—carefully—each paper, I noticed stylistic differences in Mark's F. Scott Fitzgerald paper. The writing was fluid, clear, concise, academically solid with the analysis of Fitzgerald, and extremely meticulous. When I read the metacognitive letter, I found the opposite. There was such a contrast in the two writing styles.

With this, I decided to go to the library and do some of my own research on F. Scott Fitzgerald. As I pulled the books, I leafed through each one, finding that Mark had made my work easy: he had underlined in the library book every lifted excerpt used in his paper. Writing in Mark's paper's margins, I wrote the page numbers, the books, and the authors where the excerpts were plagiarized. It was that simple, and this was before the multiple websites that are devoted to checking students' papers for plagiarism emerged.

When I returned the papers to the freshman class, I watched Mark searching through his paper, unable to locate a grade anywhere. This was, of course, intentional on my part.

I waited for a few days, waited for Mark to show up in my office.

He did.

Asking if I had forgotten to grade his paper and wondering why I did not place a grade anywhere on his work, Mark listened when I explained the writing in the margins of each page.

Mark was not a quiet student in my class, but that day he lost his voice. He looked, listened, placed his paper in his backpack, and left.

I couldn't help but think of the students who worked so hard on their papers, conducting their research honestly, analyzing what they read, and formulating their ideas from the reading they did.

In addition, I couldn't help but envision Moses coming down the mountain with two large tablets with the Ten Commandments written on them. "Thou shalt not steal" seemed to be the commandment written in bold letters that day, visible to all who viewed God's laws.

Mark was not looking.

Mark did plagiarize, knowingly and boldly. For this, no grade was given. He failed because of his act of stealing. But it just wasn't about failing the paper. It was failing himself and his fellow human beings that was the bigger sin. He disobeyed one of God's commandments.

I hope that Mark is living by the commandments today, especially the seventh commandment.

Life Lesson Learned

Each of us has duties awaiting us daily. With these duties, we must meet each one with the attitude to do our best. There are times when I wanted to find the easy way, but I have found that I must be honest, responsible, and accountable for every act I choose. From my parents I learned that whether I like doing something or not, I should face the challenge with passion and honesty. We learn from these moments in life, as James Joyce's protagonist in the literary work "The Dead" tells us: "We have all of us living duties and living affections, which claim, and rightly claim, our strenuous endeavors."[x]

Mark taught me the lesson that having passion and doing our best gives that act meaning. That's why we are here on this earth. Each of us is accountable to contributing to the human condition, and we must contribute in a positive way. No matter at what age or what duty, we give ourselves to others with courage and love. That's the secret of life: love. We must love what we do and for whom we are doing it. Only then will we live by God's commandments.

For this life lesson, I thank you, Mark.

CHAPTER 33

Sticks and Stones Will Break My Bones...

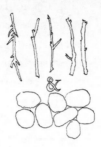

Paul's Story

She was a junior at the university and an English writing concentration major. Melanie loved English as much as I did and was not afraid to show it and to share it. Perhaps it was not the sharing; it was the showing. Immediately, I was mesmerized by the depth of her passion for the subject and its various components: the grammar, the composition, and the literature. Having the skill and competence in the subject matter, Melanie excelled above the rest. She asked questions, challenged the comments of other students, and listed a litany of academic support for her own answers and reasoning.

When we worked in collaboration within the small group context, Melanie would take the leadership role, even though there should be no leaders in a collaborative dynamic. When others tried to speak, she overruled their answers with a louder voice accompanied by a dominant look. Her long, raven hair and tall stature gave her more authority and command, along with the vast knowledge of the subject.

Yes, I was impressed with this student who was preparing to become a high school English teacher. I just didn't see what I should have seen.

During spring semester, Melanie took the Teaching Writing as a Process course from me. Her ability to incorporate the course information with the methodology in the classroom was mature and quite dynamic. She shared her talents and craft for writing and modeled the methodology with experience.

In this class was another student who was also preparing to become a high school English teacher. Paul was a good writer, working hard to acquire the information necessary for his professional career.

Until that day…

The students had to do group presentations in front of the class, reflecting class information exemplifying subject and methodology. Melanie and Paul were in different groups, avoiding potential run-ins like the ones that surfaced in class at times, until the day Paul's group presented their work to the class.

After the presentation, questions and answers followed. Melanie began to question the information, point by point. As each member of the group answered, I realized that the constant questioning masked Melanie's intent to dehumanize and embarrass. Paul seemed to be singled out and was jabbed again and again. The answers began to grow more and more silent, as if those answering were falling into a deep cavern.

I stopped the activity and thanked the group.

Years later, Paul was visiting the campus and stopped to see me in my office.

We discussed the many years that had flown by and reminisced about the course of mine he took one spring semester.

Suddenly, I heard those words: "The class was a good one, but the one student in that class destroyed my desire to contribute to any discussion, as it did for so many other students."

"Who was the student?"

But I did not even have to ask the question.

"The one student who always wanted to act like you. Melanie."

Act like me?

I felt a chill.

Act like me?

I had no words for Paul that day, no words of apology, no words seeking forgiveness, no words of explanation concerning my shallow insight into Melanie's actions and words. Somehow, I knew this even back then. *Why was I prideful, knowing that someone wanted to be just like me? I knew better.*

"Her words hurt. Her tone hurt. Her questions with the implication that what we had to offer was not worth what she could offer were offensive. Her words hurt."

Paul left that day, seeming more relaxed, more willing to express what was in his heart and on his mind. He had exhaled after so many years concerning this unwanted memory.

Probably for the first time—ever.

As I watched him leave my office, I thanked God for Paul's return.

Life Lesson Learned

I found that pride truly is one of the cardinal sins in this life. Melanie wanted to "act like me." When I saw her actions and her harshness with Paul and his group—with all the students in the class—she was "acting like me," and I did not want to look into my own soul to find what I did not want to see.

I was reminded that day with Paul that "sticks and stones will break my bones but names will never hurt me" was wrong. I was also reminded that sticks and stones may break bones if thrown hard or if thrown a certain way, but I came to realize that names *do* hurt and can destroy. Names *do* hurt and can damage a life—sometimes forever. I have become more observant of who I am in the classroom, of what I exhibit in the classroom, and of what I say not only in the classroom but with all whom I meet.

For this life lesson, I thank you, Paul.

CHAPTER 34

Never Judge a Book by Its Cover

Natalie's Story

She had long, black hair and was extremely quiet. Being new to the university campus and to the American culture, Natalie walked into her first American class, my Advanced Composition II class, that semester. I remember her well. She sat in the back of the classroom and in the back of the computer lab. We used the lab for the collaboration process of writing once a week, where students uploaded their papers and commented on one another's work.

Throughout the semester, Natalie used her notebook, her hand-formed letters representing her culture through the handwritten art unlike the stark letters of the American alphabet. She never used the computer like the other students; she wrote in pen with every letter forming an exquisite shape, shapes like peacocks.

I permitted her to use a pen and notebook for a few weeks. Nevertheless, working without a computer withdrew her from the suggestions of other students, from her suggestions to other students, from editing more easily throughout the revision process, and from being part of a community of writers in that class.

"You need to use the computer, Natalie. No one can see your work, and you are unable to read the other students' works. You need to use the computer."

She would look at me, saying nothing, and would use her pen and notebook, forming the artistic and beautiful peacock shapes representing her country.

Her writing is beautiful. Some of the letters look like peacocks and other shapes—unforgiving, not cold and hard. Yes, not cold and hard with the computer-blocked, unexciting appearance of the American alphabet and numbers.

But I continued...

"You have to try using the computer. There are students who are adept with the computer and who can help you. Just work with the class and with the others, Natalie."

She would look at me, saying nothing. And she kept writing with her peacock-shaped letters.

After a few weeks, my decision for Natalie to join the class by working through the computer forced me to tell her that the pen and notebook were no longer permitted in the computer lab.

"Come to my office later, Natalie. We have to talk about the course and its requirements."

She showed up later that day.

"I cannot use the computer."

"I'll have someone teach you how to use it, or I'll give you some points about the program we are using. The process will be easy and functional."

"It's not about learning how to use the computer. It's about protecting who I am and my culture. I want to preserve the beauty of my penmanship, the art of the letters through print. I want to create literature through the beauty of my own writing. The computer destroys the art of the letter, the shape of the letters that form words."

When she revealed this to me, I realized that her actions were not rebellious, adamant, or defiant. Her unwillingness to join the rest of the class in meeting the requirement of working through the computer in the computer lab during the writing process involving collaboration was not directed at me; instead, it was an act of protection, protection for her culture, for her language, for the beauty of the alphabet that shapes "the letters that form words."

All that time I thought she was uncooperative, undisciplined, perhaps even spoiled. I had truly misjudged this young woman, a woman who was courageous enough to protect her culture, her family, her self. There was so much more to her silence than I knew.

I finally understood.

Life Lesson Learned

"Never judge a book by its cover." My parents taught me this saying when I was young, and they reinforced it as I grew older. I just never really thought about that piece of wisdom until I met Natalie. There were so many times when I looked only at the superficialities in life, until I met her. I misread signals because I read only the cover and did not take time to reflect on the hidden meanings. I learned to stop, look, and listen when I met this student.

Natalie taught me that there is more than what is visible. There is more to life and to people than what we think we see. Life is precious, yet it is transient; it is fleeting. It's a gift; and each individual has gifts that should be recognized, respected, and dignified. These gifts cannot be demeaned, nor can they be destroyed. And we must protect them in any situation. Natalie did just that.

For this life lesson, I thank you, Natalie.

CHAPTER 35

Standing by Principles

Mario's Story

He was tall, tense, and extremely talkative. Mario would saunter into the university classroom with a confident and carefree gait. The students enjoyed his presence, and it was evident that he enjoyed theirs.

Mario was a good writer and listener. When he contributed to class discussion concerning the literary works, his analysis was insightful and interesting. Mario was having a good semester in my English composition class. And this was quite evident.

As the semester continued, the work for the research paper started, and its process progressed until the paper was due at the end of the term. There were dates for each component of the research process, and the students had to meet each date so that the final date for the finished paper would not be formidable.

Mario was doing well with his research and with meeting the dates. Collaboration continued; editing flourished, and the final day was approaching quickly.

On "the day," students carried into the room their precious cargo. They held the bundle that validated long hours of reading, reflecting, writing, editing, reviewing, proofreading, and finalizing. They were ready to empty their hands; they were ready to hand over their long, hard work. And they were both relieved and proud of their papers.

I was prepared to collect them and to grade each one.

As the last paper was collected and as each student left the classroom, Mario walked toward my desk with papers in his hands.

"This is my paper. Some of it is written, and some of it is typed. I did not have time to type the rest of it, so here it is. The wrinkled areas of the paper are from the backpack. You'll have to make sure that you don't mix up the pages, because they aren't paginated. And there is no bibliography. I need more time and will type the written pages and will do a bibliography if you give me more time. How much time can I have?"

How much time can I have? How much time can I have? I couldn't believe what I heard. The requirement of turning in the paper on time was clear. The date was repeated in class again and again, and the work was turned in piecemeal so that it would not be overwhelming at the end.

"Today is the due date, Mario, not tomorrow or any time. Everyone turned in the typed, completed paper. There is no more time."

"But I don't have all of it completed or typed."

"The paper is due today."

Suddenly, the scene changed. The tall, tense, and extremely talkative student transformed into a being I did not recognize. He was not Medusa, because I could still look him in the eyes. He was not Job, because there was no patience in his stance. And this was evident. He was neither a recognizable mythological nor biblical character. He was what I did not know.

"I can't believe that you won't take my work! It's not fair! This is unjust!" His arms waived erratically.

He walked out. He stomped out, thrusting his half-written paper, his handwritten pages, his wrinkled pages in the air. I never saw him again.

One day several years later, I was walking down the steps leading to the campus library. It was a breezy yet normal, spring day. As I walked, I couldn't help but enjoy the smiling students' faces passing me as I continued my quick journey to the building.

Suddenly, I saw a tall man approaching me. I moved toward the right so that he could pass me without trouble. He moved toward his left. I quickly moved toward the left so that he could pass. He shifted toward his right. It was apparent that he wanted to walk right into me.

I stopped. And I was afraid.

He continued to walk in front of me, a magnanimous, impenetrable wall.

"I have thought about you for years, Dr. Sunyoger, and have always wanted to meet with you when I returned to campus."

I was confused. *Who are you?*

"For years I held a grudge against you for not giving me more time to do my research paper when I was in your writing class. I did not have it finished and wanted more time. You wouldn't give it to me. I left class, angry and unforgiving, placing the blame on you and not on me. I left your class and never returned. Because of that incident, I had to leave the university. I was on academic probation from the previous semester. And failing your class gave me no choice. I was asked to leave the university, so I left.

"I joined the navy for four years and have now returned in order to work toward a degree. I never forgave you until I found that I had to be accountable for my actions and had to receive the consequences for the decisions I made in the navy. The university made me leave because of my poor class standing, so I went into the service. The navy was tough on me. But I needed the strict discipline of the service in order to understand why you stood by your principles that day in your class.

"You were protecting the other students who put in the time and who did their work. You were teaching us more than the textbook information. You were teaching us about life, and I didn't get that until I went into the world and into the navy. There, I learned that if you had backed down from your principles that day, you would have been unfair to the others in that class, to you, and to me. You did what was right, and I wanted to tell you this for so long. It took me a while to learn this. Thank you for doing this for me so many years ago. This also helped prepare me for the navy and its discipline."

I was no longer afraid.

Recognizing him from his story, I was thankful that I found out what had happened to Mario, relieved that he turned out well, that he was mature, that he was happy, that he was grateful, that he was forgiving from the wisdom he now had.

And I thanked God for giving me the strength and courage to stand by my principles that day so long ago.

Life Lesson Learned

There are times when we cannot succumb to a situation where we must sacrifice our principles when we know that we are not only defending them, but that we are defending those individuals for whom those principles were constructed. I did not like standing there that day, stating that I would not give more time for Mario to work on his research. What gave me the courage to stand by my principles were the students who turned in their papers on time. I could not be a traitor to them. So I stood by the due date, yet I never forgot Mario and wondered what had happened to him.

I thank God every day, for I can still close my eyes and see that man, a former enlisted serviceman surprisingly interrupting my journey to the library. I thank God that not only did I learn a lesson that standing by principles takes courage and strength, but that another also learned a great lesson—after some time. I also learned that Mario became stronger spiritually, that he grew closer to the divine as he saw beyond the immediate act that day in the classroom. He forgave me; perhaps he forgave himself first. By taking this holy step, his forgiveness was divine.

Alexander Pope states, "To err is human; to forgive is divine." I, too, forgave myself for questioning my act, thinking that it would be so much easier to do what others want, to sacrifice principle for comfort. Mario reinforced my firm belief that no matter how hard it may be, we must stand by principles for the dignity of others.

For this life lesson, I thank you, Mario.

CHAPTER 36

Using Brawn for Brain

Marty's Story

Marty was a non-traditional student, that is, a student who does not enter college right after high school. A non-traditional student is older than the average just-out-of-high-school college freshman. A non-traditional student has more life experiences.

Older than his classmates, Marty joined the English writing concentration majors at the university with enthusiasm and energy. Not only did he major in English, but he also minored in Computer Science, since that was his specialization while he was in the army for four years.

He was a congenial man, always smiling with curious eyes and hiding an inhibited personality. This inhibition—or low self-esteem—was his Achilles heel. His mission at the university was to keep this a secret throughout his academic journey toward acquiring a degree.

Marty was a kind man, an eager-to-learn student whom society would describe as a solitary man. Perhaps his age, his world experience, or just his introverted personality encouraged this trait. But this did not deter him from being back in the classroom and working on a Bachelor of Arts degree.

The first time I met Marty was when he registered for my Advanced Composition I course. He sat in the center row in the first seat. His curiosity about the language, literary works, and discussions that emerged from the readings engaged his attention. Although he infrequently spoke in class, when I called his name, he commented with mature insight.

The students respected him and looked up to him for his wisdom earned from having more life experiences. He remained humble and grateful as he continued to make his mark on the class. And his secret was safe.

Marty would periodically come to my office with questions about the literary works and their meanings contained "between the lines." I attributed the initial struggle with literary analysis to his connection with computers in the army, not utilizing literary analysis until the university English class. So we talked, discussed works, shared his life experiences, and he eventually became more relaxed and more secure in the classroom.

Throughout the semester, I noticed Marty always carrying a backpack bulging with books. Every time he walked into the class, he emptied most of the bag, revealing not only his textbooks but also many literary classics. His modern American books, his British literature and world literature textbooks were crammed into that backpack. I was amazed at the number of books and, apparently, the amount of reading that Marty had to be doing with a statement from his backpack like that.

He truly was a model for the traditional students. They looked up to him, respected him, couldn't deny that he worked hard, and appreciated how he valued academic work. The hard-working ethic he reflected was a good one for them to see. His statement was clear: we must work hard and cherish the opportunity given to each of us. We are never too old to develop our minds, to strive for our dreams, and to achieve our goals.

Marty's writing was developing well, and his membership into the community of readers was also becoming more and more mature and insightful with his contributions to class discussions.

Marty continued to take more and more of my English classes for his program of study, since he declared his major to be English with a concentration in writing. From the number of classes we shared and from the number of books he continuously carried when he came to class, I was certain that he would succeed in a major that had been so foreign to him initially.

He seemed at peace on campus, enjoying his time, growing in wisdom. And the secret was still safe.

One afternoon after class, Marty took longer than usual to pack his many books into his backpack. From much practice, Marty placed each book in its proper place, making room for the next occupant. Watching what seemed to be a meticulous chess game, I finally walked over to him.

"You have always carried so many books in your backpack, Marty. Ever since you arrived on this campus, you have never been without them in your pack. When do you find time to read all of those works plus the assigned texts from your classes? In addition to your major, you have your Computer Science minor and have academic work for those classes. Do you have any time for yourself?"

"I manage with the work and try to do what is required for the classes."

"Are you doing more outside reading and skipping the required class work?"

"No, I do fine with the class work."

"Do you get any rest at night, or is the reading keeping you too busy? The backpack is always so full. Could you just carry some of the texts that you need and keep the others in the dorm?"

He looked at me, and his stature suddenly seemed to become as small as a Lilliputian. His secret was safe, thus far.

I am prying too much. He is recoiling and wants to keep his life private. Yet the unnecessary carrying of all those books can be rectified by packing only the ones he needs for the classes that he attends on specific days. I was just trying to help.

Again, our eyes met. But his eyes quickly fell, covering the windows of his soul that contained a precious secret.

"I always make sure I carry books with me every day so that students will see how academically disciplined I am and will think that I am an intellectual. I do carry these books, but I have never read one of them. They are for looks; that's all. They are props so that students will see me as an intelligent adult and not as an uneducated person. This is my biggest fear. I don't want students to think that I am dumb or that they are smarter than I am. I always had that fear."

An intellectual? An intellectual? All this time, Marty carried books in his backpack as props, as if he were an actor on stage where a classroom was created and as if he were the intellectual protagonist of the story. All this time, Marty had been fighting his fear of failure. So the only way for him to work through this fear was to pretend, to feign his academic superiority.

I had no words for some time. I think I told Marty to be himself, not to live a lie, to face his fears, to reflect on his positive and negative traits, and to conquer them—one at a time. I think I told him to empty his backpack and to carry only the books he needed. I think I told him to love himself for who he was and for what he contributed to the human condition, and I think I told him to read those books someday for what they had to say because he wanted to, not because he was hiding his fear of looking "stupid," and I know I told him to believe in himself and in God.

Marty left that day, returning with a much lighter-looking backpack for the rest of his career on campus. No longer did Marty have to worry about keeping a secret safe.

Sometimes when I think of Marty after all these years, I wonder if he read any of those literary works.

I bet he did.

Life Lesson Learned

Marty taught me to look into my own self and to reflect on what I wanted others to see and on what I was hiding. He gave me the courage to empty my backpack of props and to have the courage to face my fears and to make positive changes in my life.

Sometimes we become so enamored by what we think others want to see. Sometimes we want to be accepted by others so badly that we begin to create smoke screens. Sometimes we lose ourselves in the business of living life and forget what truly is important. I realized that the process of recognizing truth and of transcending those obstacles that hinder us from seeking truth is a difficult one but one that can be attained with persistence, belief in self, and belief that all things can happen because of our faith in God. This conquers the secret.

For this life lesson, I thank you, Marty.

Chapter 37

Students and Chivalry

Jacob's Story

Jacob registered for my university Studies in Fiction course offered during the summer session, a five-week term so that he could meet his requirement for the humanities core that students needed for graduation. Summer classes were usually small, but that summer was different.

There were seventeen students in the Studies in Fiction class, which ignited great discussions about the short stories. Several students were international ones, with the majority being nontraditional. Nontraditional students usually gravitate to summer courses, since the sessions are shorter, and students can take more courses to fulfill their programs of study for their majors. These classes are demanding, since most classes meet daily with continuous nightly preparation, reading, and writing. But these smaller classes do offer a familial community and a quicker pace with classes.

Throughout the summer session, Jacob stayed focused. He always chose the center row and the center seat. Although his frame was small, Jacob's smile transformed him into a giant of a man. The attention was intense; his silence was loud; his desire to do his best was unequivocal. He was the student for whom all teachers prayed to have in class—he was the life-long learner. It showed.

Jacob not only brought his eagerness to learn into the classroom, but he brought his kindness, his dedication, and his consideration for the other students into the class. I really did not know too much about Jacob other than what I saw in the classroom; however, I saw the goodness in him and appreciated the blessing of his presence in my life.

That summer, like other summers, welcomed prospective students who visited the university campus and professors. Those eager students brought their parents who were reluctant to hand over their children just to anyone, making certain that the campuses they visited would be the perfect match for their children. Our campus was ready for the visitors.

So they came.

The designated "come-and-see" week bustled with new faces and feet that hit the cement with a staccato pace. No one knew anyone, but they became family while they visited.

One afternoon while I was walking to the student union to give a presentation to the visitors about the English department and its course offerings, I turned abruptly to see two men who were neither our students nor campus visitors (as I later found out) walking behind me, since I had sensed their urgency to catch up with me. Walking faster, I heard their pace quicken. Suddenly, I had an uncomfortable feeling. Walking even faster, I sensed their pace quickening.

I was afraid.

The student union seemed so far away, farther than it was before this moment. As my pace hastened to a slow run, I saw Jacob and his visiting uncle walking toward me. They were several yards away, but they saw the look in my eyes and the pace of my stride.

They increased their steps, flanking me with protection. The two men behind me suddenly walked away, veering off toward the right and moving off campus without turning around.

"Are you okay, Dr. Sunyoger?"

"I am now, Jacob. Thank you so much for coming to my aid. You are both so kind."

"My uncle and I realized that you were in distress and did what comes naturally. I'll see you in class tomorrow."

I'll see you in class tomorrow. How beautiful. Those innocent words against such a different scenario. How beautiful. How soothing.

We met again in class the next day, with neither one of us referencing what happened the previous day.

Our attention was focused on another short story, and the community of readers engaged in analysis. Jacob did, also.

Yes, Jacob was truly a fine student—strong in academic dedication, responsibility, and accountability. But he was more. He was a man who was chivalrous.

He was a man who was kind. He was a man who was courageous.

He recognized an individual in need and acted quickly; and for this, he removed the danger without thinking about himself. He did not look the other way.

Life Lesson Learned

My role as teacher in the classroom is to develop those individuals who sit in front of me, seeking wisdom through learning and studying. Timothy's words—"Study to prove thyself unto the Lord"[xi]—sit etched into a wooden plaque that sits on my desk. These words remind me how much learning enables us to grow closer to God in our search for Truth and Wisdom. We find the secret to life in this search: to love every single person and to stand up for each other. Never did I imagine that these words would come to life. Never did I imagine that one of my students would act quickly for another. For me!

That's what we read about in the literary works. We read about chivalry contained in the great classics. Through the kind act of another, I see beauty and goodness in this world. I feel the love of God through another human being with the willingness to "lay down one's life for another." And I recognize my own worth and value through Jacob's act that one summer day.

Today, Jacob is a priest, and I envision him dignifying everyone around him and saving souls.

For this life lesson, I thank you, Jacob.

CHAPTER 38

What's in a Grade?

George's Story

Establishing a set of guidelines—a rubric for the evaluation of students' papers—challenges me every semester, every year. Throughout my years of teaching, being "just and fair" navigated me—and continues to navigate me—when I re-assess and re-evaluate my previous rubrics. But my first few years of university teaching found me to be unseasoned—even with creating a rubric.

But I did not let this deter me. I confidently revised my former rubrics semester after semester, updating some of the points addressing both the content and the mechanics of a paper. My work covered every nook and cranny—or so I thought.

With one particular new rubric, I was prepared to meet the new school year. It was spring semester, and my students were rested, alert, and eager to learn after their long Christmas break as they embarked on another academic journey. Walking into the classroom with *the* rubric in hand that first day of class, I defined it and explained its purpose. The students listened and accepted the rubric and its restrictions without questions or complaints.

I wish they had questioned and complained.

For each paper we used the rubric like a Bible. Never losing sight of what good writing is, the students utilized the information throughout the writing process.

Grades were dropped because of the students' negligence, unawareness, or simply laziness in working on developing themselves as writers. Consistent with its use, I never wavered from the guidelines in the rubric.

But…I should have.

Seated in the second row, first desk was a young man who was an English writing concentration major. The love he had for writing and literature was evident as he sought answers, contributed to class discussions, offered suggestions to his peers in the collaboration process, and constantly worked hard to improve his writing from paper to paper.

George demanded his best and performed his best. And he lived by this with every assignment and class activity that term.

Before the end of the semester, students faced the final assignment—the research paper. Working for weeks, researching, drafting, and editing, the students met the due day for the research assignment, knowing that it would be graded according to my rubric they had been given at the beginning of the semester.

George reflected relief and confidence. His papers always met the criteria stated on the rubric. He never had trouble with the mechanics; his content always reflected mature insight and academic thought. Always receiving the highest grades, George still remained humble and willing to take more constructive criticism so that he could improve as a writer. He wanted to grow in knowledge and wisdom.

His research did not disappoint me. His insight did not disappoint me, and his style did not disappoint me.

But the grade disappointed me.

As I read his work, his hard work, I found a misspelled word—one misspelled word, causing his paper to drop to a C minus. The grade was unfair, unjust, and merciless. I knew that, but I remembered my rubric.

One misspelled word immediately drops the paper to a C minus.

My rubric demanded that I would adhere to the spelling criterion. For the entire semester, I dropped grades for misspelling. But the papers with misspelled words contained many misspelled words and other writing errors. George's paper housed only one.

I reread my rubric. *One misspelled word immediately drops the paper to a C minus.* There was no escape for me. George's fate was determined by this rubric rule. So I did what was one of my worst professional acts: I placed the C⁻ at the end of the lengthy and well-written work with remorse.

When I returned the papers to the class, I watched George's face as he read my annotations in the margins of his paper—page by page. A smile would emerge; a glint of excitement would appear in his eyes, and an excited hand would turn the pages. As he approached the last page, the world stopped: both his world and mine.

The smile disappeared; the glint of excitement faded; the hands shook. The engaged, enthusiastic student disappeared. But George was not destroyed. He would never be destroyed. And this is where strength lies. George continued to demand his best throughout the rest of his time with me—and with the rubric. Like Hemingway's Santiago in *The Old Man and the Sea*, man's greatness is presented and praised. This selflessness and learning from undesired experiences is what strengthens us. Yes, we may be defeated by the tragedies in life, but we will not let them destroy us. Instead, we will rise–renewed—like the phoenix, like Santiago, like George.

George received his paper that day with humility. The rubric was clear. George did not question or complain.

I wish he had.

The path he chose to take was one of trusting my judgment without being destroyed. Knowing this made me even more ashamed.

The criterion under mechanics stating that, "one misspelled word immediately drops the paper to a C minus" was removed from the rubric at the end of that spring semester. Never again would I evaluate a paper based on one minor point, denying a paper's content, the writer's style, and a student's academic research and genuine hard work.

One misspelled word…

To this day, I remember this incident as if it happened this morning. To this day, I regret the decision I made, not being fair and just to this student and to those students who preceded him.

Our time together ended. We both moved on, living our lives. I am certain that George learned never to misspell that word again, but I became the wiser, recognizing that some rules that are unjust must simply not be followed.

I never included that rule again.

And I hope that George, who is now a priest, has absolved me and has personally forgiven me for my action.

Life Lesson Learned

George taught me the virtue of control, of patience, of love. He grew from that situation, gaining insight and wisdom. In addition, his accountability for breaking the rule that served all students in the evaluation process was evident. He accepted his consequence for his action. George taught me to be careful when establishing rules. I learned more about fairness and justice that day. And I have grown in the wisdom of knowing how to stand by these virtues. I needed George to remove the plank in my eye, to eradicate the blindness, and to help me recognize what I need to do when I set an unfair standard. "What's in a grade?" you ask. Too much at times. Too much.

For this life lesson, I thank you, George.

Chapter 39

Coincidence?

Lana's Story

I always tell my future teachers to respect those students who are assertive, but I warn my future teachers that they must know the difference between assertion and aggression from their students. Teachers should help students diffuse aggression before it erupts. This is dangerous and unacceptable both in the classroom and in the world.

Students must be encouraged to feel comfortable approaching a teacher if they have a question or if they suspect unfairness. In return, teachers must give students opportunities to be assertive in seeking these answers. Along with this belief, I also feel that any incident in life is not a coincidence. It is a "God incident," a situation we experience that determines our choice either to grow or remain stagnant. We have the power to handle these incidents with assertion or aggression.

And this should be with everyone, not just with students. Situations demand that choices be made.

Lana belonged to neither the aggression community nor the assertion community.

As a freshman taking her first English composition course at the university, Lana's quiet personality contained a secret compartment of energy and excitement for academia. She was a gifted writer, a strong student, a good person. Her respect for the opportunity to learn and to work toward a college degree was apparent, and her ability to do the work was unquestionable.

Lana's was a joy to teach.

The semester moved quickly, as each one always does. Soon the term ended, and the students left my classroom, taking other courses to fulfill their programs of study for their selected majors. I never saw Lana again in my classes, since she was an Education major, taking courses that would prepare her for her profession.

I knew that she would succeed. She had the desire to learn, the compassion for others, and the personality that engages individuals. The quiet side of her personality intensified the qualities that helped her connect with the students in my class. Her future students would find her passion for teaching contagious and would grow from her own educational and life nourishment. Yes, she would be good for her students, and they would be good for her. Wishing her well, I said good-bye that semester.

One afternoon, three years later, I, as always, was using the back stairwell to exit the building where my office is located. There are very few students in that section of the building, since most students do not seem to know that there is an exit door there.

More faculty than students use that stairwell, so it is unusual for teachers to run into students on the stairs. Students like the activity of noise, conversation, and elbow-to-elbow walking to and from their classes. There is none of that in that section of the building.

I was consistent with that path. I no longer needed breadcrumbs to lead the way to and from my office. Every day's walk was the same—except that day, I experienced a "God incident."

Walking down the steps that afternoon, I heard footsteps behind me. Turning around and expecting to see a colleague, I saw a student who looked somewhat familiar.

"Are you finished with classes for the day?" I asked, initiating conversation.

"Yes."

"You look familiar. Do I know you?"

"I took your freshman English composition class when I was a freshman. This is my senior year, and I will be teaching in the fall."

"What is your name?"

"Lana."

"I remember you, Lana. You were in my English 103 morning class. I remember how well you wrote."

Her pupils turned into question marks. "You did not think that then."

"What do you mean?"

"I received a D for that course."

I was like a Skylander in our world, frozen, praying for the portal that would give me life.

"I did not give you a D. You were one of my best students in that class. I remember."

"But I did receive a D."

She was kind, non-aggressive, and only informative. Her velvet words gave her voice a smooth flow of syllables in my world of silence surrounded by confusion.

"Lana, I need to look into this. Why didn't you come to me three years ago when you received the D?"

"I didn't want you to think that I was being disrespectful by coming to you. You might have thought that I was arguing with you. I thought I deserved the grade."

I thought I deserved the grade! I thought I deserved the grade! I thought I deserved the grade?

"You should have come to see me. You should have been assertive and questioned the grade. We need to do that in life when we have a question about anything. We must question. That's the only way we can find out if what has occurred is fair and just. Please, learn to be assertive, to question, and to defend what you know is right."

I looked into the grade—from three years ago. An error occurred as the grade was transferred from my grade sheet to the computer. The original grade metamorphosed into something else. I could not fathom Lana's choice of being quiet instead of being assertive since she thought I would tag her as being aggressive.

The change was quick and easy. But it took three years to correct the error.

Recalling that day when I walked down the stairs with a former student, I know that this was no coincidence. It was a "God incident" where truth emerged, where a situation had to be corrected.

Where an incorrect grade had to be addressed.

It was only moral. It was only right.

I thanked God then for the chance to take care of a matter that held as much importance in my life as it did in Lana's life. I thank God now that He gave us the opportunity to meet again.

I pray that this "God incident" helped Lana become assertive.

God would not want her any other way.

And I thank Him for that.

Life Lesson Learned

There is no such thing as coincidence. What happens in life is for a reason, and it is our responsibility to listen, to reflect, and to find out what the reason is. Then we must choose to become a better person because of the incident or to succumb to it. A "God incident" is unexpected. From these incidents, assertion brings empowerment and strength, although we must be concerned about not stepping over the line from assertion to aggression.

Lana taught me to be assertive by going to the registrar's office and finding a way to check over the grades placed on those grade sheets. Lana taught me to be kind, gentle, and compassionate when being assertive. Lana also taught me to check and re-check my work. Although that takes more time, this is necessary. Whenever we think that an incident is a coincidence, we must stop and reflect on why it happened. It is a "God incident," and we must learn from it.

For this life lesson, I thank you, Lana.

CHAPTER 40

The Gift of Giving

Rose's Story

My students waited for me to walk into the university classroom that morning. Rose, as usual, was sitting in the middle of the classroom in the front seat. As always, her eyes were riveted on me as I began the class with the Our Father and proceeded with the lecture for that day. I expected no surprises, but was I wrong!

After class one day, I told Rose and a few students about a rosary that I had cherished for years. A red-beaded rosary blessed by the blessed Pope John Paul II had been given to me by a student who visited the Holy Pontiff in Rome and who had it blessed by the pontiff. Receiving this rosary as a gift from one of my students made the rosary so special, and my love for the pope gave the rosary even more meaning. I carried the rosary with me everywhere; I prayed on that rosary daily.

A few years after I had received the rosary, someone asked me for a rosary blessed by the pope for a woman who was dying from several brain tumors. The woman was young and had two children. At first I was surprised at the request, but I couldn't refuse.

I relinquished my rosary—reluctantly. No longer praying on those cherished beads, I reintroduced myself to my retired white-beaded rosary.

So again, I prayed on my old rosary beads, praying for the new owner and wondering how she was doing. In time, I heard she had peacefully passed from this life.

And my red-beaded rosary had been buried with her.

This is the story I told Rose, stating that I did miss my rosary, although I knew that the rosary had given its new owner peace, so much peace that she had it buried with her.

One day toward the end of the semester, Rose stayed after class for a moment. I always enjoyed talking with Rose after class or in my office. She was a good person, a personable young woman, and a dedicated student. She led class discussions, assisted students with their writing development in collaborative settings, and created a comfortable and pleasant climate in the classroom.

She was simply a joy to have in class. And her classmates reflected those same feelings.

"Dr. Sunyoger, I have something for you."

This conversation I didn't expect. We usually discussed some points that had been covered in class.

"What do you mean?"

"Over the break, I went to Rome with my parents and had an audience with Pope Benedict XVI. While I was there, I found this and remembered your story about the red-beaded rosary. I had this blessed by the pope. Although it wasn't blessed by the blessed Pope John Paul II, it still has a pope's blessing."

She stretched out her arm and opened her hand, revealing a beautiful red-beaded rosary.

"My rosary, Rose! This is just like my red-beaded rosary. Thank you. Thank you."

I do recall telling Rose that every time I would pray the rosary, I would include her and her petitions in my prayers. But I was so surprised, excited, and shocked that I don't remember anything else I said.

But I won't ever forget Rose, her thoughtfulness, and her kindness.

And, yes, I still have my red-beaded rosary. And to this day, every time I say the rosary, I include Rose and her petitions with mine.

Perhaps this rosary will be buried with me when it is my turn. It gives me that much peace.

Life Lesson Learned

What we give comes back to us a hundredfold. I am a witness to this saying. Teaching involves the gift of giving: the gift of self. Every teacher must recognize the importance of teaching and the responsibility of touching students' lives. For teaching is a moral activity that gives teachers the responsibility of helping students see what they can do when they don't think they can. Yes, teaching is a moral activity, and this is what I have used as my compass throughout my teaching, both in and out of the classroom.

Rose gave me the window that I peered through that day, learning that by telling life stories—everyday stories about beauty, stories about the human condition, stories about love and honesty—that these stories change people's lives. In my case, the red-beaded rosary story was told without any expectation that it would produce an outcome. I simply wanted to share it. And it did become extraordinary. Not only did I learn that students listen to what is taught in the classroom, but I also learned that they listen to what teachers share outside the classroom. When we give out of pure love and expect nothing in return, we receive God's bountiful blessings. That's what makes the ordinary acts become extraordinary.

For this life lesson, I thank you, Rose.

CHAPTER 41

Home Is Where the Heart Is

Sylvia's Story: A Story of Family

I credit myself for remembering my childhood. Perhaps the memories have been somewhat tweaked at this age; perhaps they are untouched by memory loss. But what I do remember quite vividly from my only house in which I grew up was the plaque on the wall above the kitchen sink.

The plaque was stationed in the center and overshadowed every knickknack that resided there. Made from metal that was painted brown with red letters that matched the red plastic tiles and yellow plastic tiles bordering the entire kitchen, the plaque proudly stated, "Home is where the heart is."

I loved looking at those words, not knowing what they said or meant until I learned how to read, but knowing that they were special. My parents were those words. They gave my siblings and me a home—not just a house. Yes, my father built the house, brick by brick. He laid the floor, plumbed, wired for electricity, and poured his unconditional love and loyalty into his family through it all.

The house was connected with cement.

My family was glued together with love.

My brother, sister, and I never realized that we were poor by society's standards; instead, we knew we were rich in the love and sacrifices given to us by our parents.

We quickly understood the meaning of those words resting on that plaque; our parents' hearts made that house our home.

Growing up, we appreciated the opportunities offered to us by our parents. The gift of a college education was their sacrifice for each of us. That's what made it so special, and that's why my siblings and I never took school for granted. Being second-generation Italian-Americans, we appreciated our mother staying home to care for us and our father working two jobs in order to meet the financial demands of raising a family.

Three children had a choice of going to college, and all three children accepted the opportunity, unrelenting in the journey whose finish line was the bachelor's degree.

But the degree had a price—three price tags that demanded more hard work and more sacrifices.

Until each of the three children received a degree.

Throughout the hard work during those years of our schooling, our mother and father never asked for anything in return, only for us to do our best, to protect the family name, to be peaceful in our professional and personal lives, to do goodness in this life, and to love God.

We listened and learned.

The day came—as it does in a family's life—for the children to leave as adults and to begin their own lives.

So we left and built our own homes while practicing what we learned. We carried our education and faith into the world with humility and gratitude. We thanked God for the parents He gave us. We promised our parents that we would make them proud, and we promised our God that He would be pleased with how we would live our lives. We left, my brother and sister beginning their lives in Arizona. I left but stayed in town, building my home like the one I had been blessed with so many years ago, for I knew that home is where the heart is.

As I began and continued with my career, I realized more and more my mother's and father's personal sacrifices. Mom always wanted to go to college but never had the chance. She took care of her own mother who had lost a leg from diabetes and who needed assistance during her remaining years. When my mother married my father, she began to raise three children, making certain that our clothes were clean, that we took music lessons, that we had food on the table, always emulating through these actions the words on the welcomed kitchen visitor—the plaque that oversaw the Italian culture in the kitchen. Mom was our home.

Throughout all of this, Mom never thought about her desires, her dreams, and her wants. She set them aside for her family; and so did Dad, as he worked two jobs daily, yet he always came home at night so tired but with enough energy to play with his children. After a long, hard work day, Dad would wake us and would suddenly transform into a horse that rode all three hysterically laughing children on his back, with my sister always falling off, since she sat at the end.

We couldn't wait for the "horsey ride" promised to us from Dad's return home, even though we were already "tucked in" for the night.

When I began teaching in higher education after ten years of high school teaching, I asked my mother if she wanted to attend my university class every Monday evening. It was a business and technical writing class, and Mom accepted my offer with excitement.

I knew she would.

For several weeks, Mom would go with me and attend the class.

Covering the strategies and rules of this genre, the course material comprised memorandum writing, periodic reports, and analytical proposals, with a variety of other types of writing. Mom always took an interest in my major, revealing her innermost dream, at times, to me: she had wanted to go to business college after high school. But Mom took care of her diabetic mother, married my father, and raised three children, always setting her life aside so that we could live our lives and fulfill our dreams. Mom's unfulfilled dream of getting an education became dried up, like the dream in Langston Hughes' "A Dream Deferred." [xii]

The reason for this unfulfilled dream? Life got in the way.

So having her children grown and on their own, Mom was ready to catch her falling star and pin it to the sky.

Every Monday evening I stopped for Mom, driving her to campus. With her portfolio in hand, Mom humbly walked into the classroom, taking the last seat, middle row. She had never been in a college classroom before, so classroom literacy was foreign to her.

But that did not keep her from going to class.

I enjoyed seeing my mother in the classroom, her beaming, beautiful smile greeting me every time I locked eyes with hers. She was the embodiment of goodness, of beauty; and when I was with her, I was always home.

She was the heart of the family.

One evening while I was driving to class, Mom said, in the voice that belongs only to a mother, "Don't call on me to read my memo."

Our assignment for that week was to write a business memo that we would share with the class for suggestions.

"Why not? You worked so hard on that assignment all week. You should be proud of it."

"Please. Don't call on me."

Why wouldn't Mom want me to call on her after working with her, answering her questions, and discussing the writing in conjunction with the text all week? It didn't make sense. It just didn't make sense. For years, in fact, all of her life, Mom wanted to go to college. I don't think that it really mattered what she would have selected as a major. Mom just wanted to go to college and be a part of the classroom dynamic.

"I will call on you so that you can receive the feedback from the other students. It's good to receive comments so that your editing will be more insightful."

"I don't want you to call on me."

And…that was that!

Assignments were given; weeks passed, and Mom continued to sit in the last seat, middle row with her soul reflecting through her smile as it continuously greeted me, reminding me of the kitchen plaque: home is where the heart is.

The heart of the family—*my* family—sat before me, watching me doing what both she and Dad sacrificed out of love for me to attain.

As I watched my mother watching me, I thanked God for my parents.

The midterm exam, the perennial visitor during any college semester, approached quickly for us, so we began the preparation and countdown. Its visit was approaching.

If only I had checked her notebook…if only I had checked her notebook.

I still hear those words echoing in my head.

Mom sat that night for the midterm, working for two-and-a-half hours on the exam. She never raised her head. Her classmates did the same.

Then the time was up.

"Turn in the blue books along with the test paper on your way out."

Grading those exams would be like any other evening of grading exams, or so I thought. Evaluating each student's answers, I finally found my mother's blue book in my hands. Reading Mom's responses challenged my integrity as a professor. *She's my mother* pounded in my soul. But it was inevitable. I had to place the grade in the back of the blue book, just as I had with the other students' books.

But this grade was an F.

Reaching the last page of her blue book of answers, I reluctantly wrote…

Yes, it was an F. My own mother received an F from me, her daughter, the child for whom she sacrificed all of her life in order to give her daughter a college education, to give her daughter the life of doing what she loved, who deferred her own dreams for her children, who gave her daughter the gift of love, the gift of faith, and the gift of God, who gave her children a home where the heart is.

That evening I watched my mother's face as I distributed the exams. Her eyes remained fixed; her face stayed calm; her smile flashed. She read my words and closed the book, again focusing on my teaching for the rest of the class and for the rest of the semester.

On the way home, I asked Mom about her notes in her notebook.

"What notes did you take during the class sessions, and how did you review for the exam?"

"I never took any notes, so I didn't have anything to review for the exam."

"What? Why didn't you take any notes?"

"I didn't take notes, because I did not want to take my eyes off of you. If I had taken notes, I wouldn't have been able to watch you while you were teaching."

"Why did you want to watch me, Mom? You needed to take notes in order to study for the midterm exam."

"I had to watch you, honey. I wanted to see how you used the education that your Dad and I were able to offer you. I just wanted to watch you in the classroom."

She wanted to watch me. She wanted to watch me. She did not want to take the time away from watching me by taking notes.

She wanted to watch her daughter while her daughter taught. My mother and father sacrificed to pay for my education so that I would be a teacher and do what I loved: *teach.* They did not have money to send me to college but worked hard to get it.

My dad was blue collar. My mom stayed home and took care of three children. In society's eyes, they were not materially successful. In society's eyes, they were ordinary. But in our eyes, they were the everyday heroes who gave their lives for their children—with their hearts. This is what made them extraordinary. Their every act reflected the goodness and the beauty of their souls. They gave us all of this and more. They gave us family and a home where the heart is.

To this day when I think about my mom sitting in my classroom, I can't believe that I gave her an F on the midterm exam. She was not even registered for the course. She merely wanted to be a part of the academic community, even for just a short time, to help her understand what she and her husband sacrificed so much for in order to give her daughter a life of love, passion, and happiness in what her daughter always wanted to do: *teach*.

She received the grade graciously that day, and never said a harsh word about it. My mother lived her life for her children, and she accepted her unfulfilled dreams for her children's fulfilled dreams. This is what my father and mother did for us. For a semester my mother entered into my academic world, refusing to take notes for a good grade on a midterm so that she could watch me teach.

And she was proud.

The gift of life, the gift of faith, the gift of family, the gift of love are the gifts that diminish all others. To this day when I narrate this story, I reflect in horror what I did, although I know that this act was not a malicious one. My parents taught me virtue. We didn't know how to be malicious.

Every now and then as I look at my students sitting in front of me taking notes, I catch a glimpse of a lovely woman sitting in the middle row in the last seat with a smile full of heart and eyes full of love, as she never once drops her head. She watches me doing what I love to do. She watches me use the gift of an education that she and my father gave me with so much sacrifice and unconditional love.

The F on the midterm was unimportant. Mom always wanted to go to school and learn; instead, her children went to college and learned.

And that was what was important to Mom and Dad.

The F on the midterm was unimportant. The sacrifice Mom and Dad made in order to watch me teach was worth it for her. This was reflected in her eyes. Her love was punctuated with her every word and action.

And Mom brought HOME into my classroom. She was my heart. With her, we had our home.

I miss my mom and dad.

Life Lesson Learned

We teach love without words through our actions. My parents' love defined them as extraordinary parents who lived ordinary lives doing extraordinary things. And they left us extraordinary memories. Being my student for a semester and experiencing college life for several weeks, my mother was grateful for that opportunity. In the classroom is where family is created; in the home is where family begins.

Deceased now, my parents no longer can hear their children's words of gratitude and love or see their children doing what they love to do, but my siblings and I continue to thank Mom and Dad by the way we live our lives. We have learned that home is where the heart is. And this is what we must pass on from generation to generation.

God created us out of His love. Life is a gift from a loving God, and we must live it that way. We must bring home to others. We must be family. Yes, my mother always knew that F is not for failure; it is for forgiveness, and it took me a long time to forgive myself for placing that F on my mother's exam booklet. Mom didn't have to forgive me. She understood. She understood that F also stands for family. That's how she lived her life; that's how both of my parents lived their lives. They gave us a home full of heart—full of love.

And I thank God for this.

And for this life lesson, I thank you, Mom and Dad.

Epilogue

This book is a tribute to my students, for they have touched my life and have taught me about myself. They have helped me enter into the depths of my soul, seeking answers to life's eternal questions.

I initially thought that I was the only one doing the teaching in my classroom. But over the years, I quickly learned the opposite. My students became my teachers; they enabled me to grow, to become a better person because they were in my life.

What my students have given me I have shared with others as I pass these life lessons on to all whom I meet. My life has been blessed by these students; their contributions have filled my soul with goodness, beauty, and truth. Because of their lives, my life has been changed.

Consequently, I wanted to write this book as a tribute to those students who graced my high school classroom and my university classroom over these past forty-one years.

However, these narratives represent only a small portion of my experiences and a small number of the thousands of students I have taught for so many years. To all of them, I ask for their forgiveness for not including them in this work. To all of them, I give my gratitude, and I celebrate them for their contributions in bringing me to this place of who I am and of what I have become.

I hope that in some small way I have enabled them to become better individuals through my teaching.

My promise to all of my students is that I shall never forget them. I may not remember some names, but I shall never forget their legacy. I may not remember the year they were in my class, but I shall never forget the face, the smile, the gift of themselves that they brought with them. I may not remember their grade, but I shall never forget the wisdom that emerged from the connection of our souls as we journeyed through the learning together.

To these students, I thank them for letting me into their lives. They gave me permission to be a part of their lives, to be part of their family.

Some of these narratives occurred forty-one years ago; others occurred last semester. Yet each one I can recall without any struggle. They are so vivid.

The intention behind the writing of this book is to share with my readers the happiness I have received from my career. In return, I hope that others take these narratives to help them recall their own stories. Each of us has an arsenal of experiences that develop us into who we are and into what we do. We must reflect on our lives touched by so many, making our world a better place for having entered into one another's life.

What has become the cornerstone of your life? Which experience stands out the most for you, has the most meaning for you, has touched your life, and has changed your soul?

These are the reasons for this book of short narratives. I have not seen most of these individuals for years, yet they live in my heart. I pray that they are blessed with individuals in their lives who will give them what they have given me. I pray that they are blessed abundantly for the goodness that they do. I pray for a life of peace, happiness, love, and a deep faith in family and God for each one of them.

From my own family, I learned life-long virtues and developed a deep love for family and a strong faith in God. My parents taught my brother, sister, and me how to live life with laughter and with a passion for what we do. They taught us about God by giving us the gift of faith. They were our first teachers.

My students had their families. But as their teacher, I also was entrusted to discuss virtue, to discuss contributing to society and caring for one another. That's what families do. That's what the classroom— the extension of family—should do.

But I was not the only one teaching. I was *their* teacher, but my students were *my* teachers. They challenged me to think, to reflect, and to prepare my own life for eternal life. They deepened my childhood virtues. My students gave me their love, allowing me to enter into their lives.

I don't know how many students there have been. But I do know that every student changed my life.

My parents made it possible for me to meet these individuals in the classroom, students God chose for me to meet and for them to meet me—from the beginning of time. I thank God for that gift. I thank my mom and dad for that gift. And…

I thank you, dear students, all of you. You know who you are. All of you have touched and contributed to my life. God has blessed me, truly blessed me, for having had the chance to meet each one of you, for having shared our lives, for having connected our souls.

Those who were in my high school and university classes are today's doctors, dentists, mayors, police officers, accountants, nurses, administrators, teachers, professors, priests, religious; they are the veterinarians, pilots, chemists, business owners, engineers, architects, and more. They are the contributors to the human condition.

Thank you for contributing to the goodness of society.

Thank you for passing down those virtues.

Thank you for passing down your selves.

You shall never be forgotten. I still hold on to your stories with gratitude and love. My life is full of blessings, because of each one of *you*.

May God bless you, and some day we shall meet again.

God bless,
Miss Gallo, aka Mrs. Sunyoger,
aka Dr. Mary Antoinette Gallo Sunyoger

The Lesson Learned
(Dedicated to Dr. Sunyoger)

She runs on pure current,
    this electric lady
Of precision and paradox.

Her passion is language,
    120 volts of
Straight diction plugged
    Into your heart.

Don't worry! All those
    Excited sentences
Of semantics will fine-
    tune their meaning
into your mind like…
    morse code:
Tap, Tap, Tappety-tap.

Stray beats? Never, so you
    had better pay
Attention in her class!

She draws you in with a
    lightning smile
To any field of concentration
    She hums by.

Lose the lingo, she sings and
    holds the last note
With shocking-green eyes—a
    gypsy-wise gaze of

Open curiosity about YOU;
      spell it: Y-O-U
Are important! That's the
      perspective!
Learn it!
      Hold it!
            Love it!

Of course, you do and you have
      just been plugged into
The right receptacle. Y-O-U are
      important and Y-O-U
Want to learn m-o-r-e…"More?"
      M*O*R*E

What properly conditioned American
      can resist the lure,
That sing-a-song lure of the
      infamous, tantalizing,
Mouth-opening, long "O"…"MORE?"

So, who is she, this electric lady
      of precision and paradox?
She's a teacher who taught me m-o-r-e
      than the meaning of words.

She taught me the meaning of life!
      For every smile she flashed
Across the tears in her soul…she
      Taught me how to keep
Adversity that had turned to m-o-r-e
      Turn from becoming

t-o-o m-u-c-h!

She is a lady of pure current and
    her source is love
From a higher power. She's someone
    who taught me a lesson
That I forgot to tell her she had
    TAUGHT!

Please accept my thanks, Dr. Sunyoger.
    It is one semester late.
Just remember, I did turn in m-o-s-t
    Of my homework on time…

May God bless you even as you have
    blessed me and so many
Others! Exceptional people weather
    exceptional circumstances,
A lesson you taught me with your smile
    across the tears.

I wonder, electric lady of precision and
    paradox, do you know
Just how much the world needs your gypsy-
    wise gaze, your lightning smile?
And your passion for language and life?

        —Your grateful student,
            Carol

Life Lesson Learned

This poem was given to me on February 3, 1989, by a student who had taken my class the previous Fall Semester. My mother passed away during that Fall Semester 1988, and Carol walked the journey of pain and loss with me, as did all of my students who were with me during that term. The tears that filled my eyes and soul were evident to my students as I walked into class, as I tried to teach while I watched my mother, my beautiful mother, die. Teaching could not conceal my raw, chafed, bleeding soul. Since then, I have, at times, questioned whether I taught well during that Fall Semester 1988, as I struggled with my mother's death. The following Spring Semester 1989, I received this poem and kept it over the years, reading it again and again as I met more pain and tears while watching my loving father, a World War II veteran, a gentle giant, and a recipient of Alzheimer's cruelty during his final stages of life, die twenty-two years later. The poem reminds me that we do connect with one another and that our connection with God through our faith in Him helps us rise above the pain and enables us to see pain and suffering as salvific, moving us forward—better, wiser—throughout life's journey. I received another mini-epiphany from Carol's poem, a strong validation, that teaching is a vocation, a gift, a connection of souls throughout life's journey. I guess I did teach during that term—throughout it all. You told me so, Carol.

For this life lesson, I thank you, Carol.

End Notes

i   These three authors discuss the importance of the classroom dynamic as a motivational force as a necessary ingredient in the writing classroom.

ii   Louise Rosenblatt elevates the responsibility of the teacher to a virtuous and more noble level: the level of morality.

iii   Nell Noddings is an educator and philosopher who coined the term "The Ethic of Caring" as a powerful component in creating a risk-free and comfortable classroom environment.

iv   Rudyard Kipling's "Gunga Din," v: 1-9.

v   *The Hollow Men*. Section V: final four verses

vi   Matthew 25:13-31

vii   This is simply one of many of Kennedy's memorable lines, taken from his January 20, 1961 Inaugural Address.

viii   Jessie Jackson said this at the 1984 Democratic National Convention in his Address.

ix   Shakespeare's tragedy *Macbeth*, 1.1.10.

x   "The Dead" is a chapter from Joyce's *Dubliners*.

xi   This is from 2 Timothy 2:15.

xii   Hughes presents the philosophical point concerning what happens to a dream if one does not pursue it. This is a reflection of one universal aspect of the human condition.

Works Cited

Eliot, T.S. "The Hollow Men." 1925. Print.

Hughes, Langston. *Montage of a Dream Deferred*. NY: Holt, 1951. Print.

Jackson, Jessie. "1984 Democratic National Convention Address." *American Rhetoric: Top 100 Speeches*. 11 November 2012. <*http://www.americanrhetoric.com /speeches/jessiejackson1984dnc.htm*>.

Joyce, James. "The Dead." *Dubliners*. New York: Dover Publications, INC.: 1991. Print.

Kennedy, John F. "Ask Not" Inaugural Address, January 20, 1961.

Kipling, Rudyard. "Gunga Din." *Poetry of the Victorian Period*. Jerome Buckley and George Woods. Scott, Foresman and Company, 1965. 892-893. Print.

Kirby, Dan, Kirby, Dawn, and Tom Liner. *Inside Out: Strategies for Teaching Writing*. NH: Heinemann, 2003. Print.

Noddings, Nel. *Educating Moral People: A Caring Alternative to Character Education*. VT: Teachers College Press, 2002. Print.

Parable of the Talents. Matthew 25: 13-31. Print.

Rosenblatt, Louise M. *Literature as Exploration.* New York: Appleton-Century, 1968. Print.

Shakespeare, William. *Macbeth. The Complete Signet Classic.* Ed. Sylvan Barnet. San Diego: Harcourt Brace Jovanovich, 1972. 1227-1261. Print.

2 Timothy 2:15